JIMMY LEE TILLMAN II

Tillman's Handbook of Great Black American Patriots

and Guide to the National Parks and Landmarks, Statues, Museums, and Historic Places dedicated to them

First published by Tillman Family Press 2021

Copyright © 2021 by Jimmy Lee Tillman II

All rights reserved. No part of this publication may be reproduced, stored or transmitted in any form or by any means, electronic, mechanical, photocopying, recording, scanning, or otherwise without written permission from the publisher. It is illegal to copy this book, post it to a website, or distribute it by any other means without permission.

Jimmy Lee Tillman II asserts the moral right to be identified as the author of this work.

Jimmy Lee Tillman II has no responsibility for the persistence or accuracy of URLs for external or third-party Internet Websites referred to in this publication and does not guarantee that any content on such Websites is, or will remain, accurate or appropriate.

Designations used by companies to distinguish their products are often claimed as trademarks. All brand names and product names used in this book and on its cover are trade names, service marks, trademarks and registered trademarks of their respective owners. The publishers and the book are not associated with any product or vendor mentioned in this book. None of the companies referenced within the book have endorsed the book.

Painting of Crispus Attucks on cover by artist George Gaadt at www.gaadtstudio.com. Back cover photo of National Afro American Musuem & Cultural Center in Wilberforce, Ohio.

First edition

ISBN: 978-1-7375214-0-2

Editing by Ebony Tillman
Cover art by Ebony Tillman

This book was professionally typeset on Reedsy.
Find out more at reedsy.com

This book is dedicated to past, present, and future graduates of Mollison Elementary and Hyde Park Career Academy in Chicago; Central State University and Wilberforce University in Wilberforce, Ohio; the men of Centralforce 124, Wilberforce #21, and Lincoln Chapter #2 (RAM); the Mighty Out Cold Crew; and to you, Keith Robinson and the Robinson Family.

"Patriotism consists not in a mere professed love of country, the place of one's birth – an endearment to the scenery, however delightful and interesting, of such country; nor simply the laws and political policy by which such country is governed; but a pure and unsophisticated interest felt and manifested for man – an impartial love and desire for the promotion and elevation of every member of the body politic, their eligibility to all the rights and privileges of society…"

Maj. Martin R. Delany

Contents

Preface iv
Acknowledgement vi

I Great Black American Patriots

1. Crispus Attucks: American Revolutionary War leader and hero — 3
2. Benjamin Banneker: Colonial Era American genius — 9
3. James Armistead Lafayette: Washington's top spy that helps... — 16
4. Phillis Wheatley: Colonial Era influencer — 23
5. Prince and Primus Hall: Father/Son Colonial Army heroes — 29
6. Peter Salem and other Black Patriots: Heroes on Bunker Hill — 37
7. Richard Allen: Early American Christian pioneer and first... — 48
8. Harriet Tubman: Presidential advisor and Civil War top spy — 56
9. Frederick Douglass: Ambassador, Union army recruiter, U.S.... — 64
10. Robert Smalls: Civil War pilot, sea captain & Republican... — 75
11. Major Dr. Alexander T. Augusta: Free man and Civil War... — 83

12 Greenbury Logan: Alamo War hero who fought for Texas... 90
13 Hendrick Arnold: Leader and spy during Texas Revolution 96
14 Major Dr. Martin Delany: Civil War strategist, inventor,... 102
15 Dr. Mary McLeod-Bethune: Advisor to the president, civic... 109
16 Monroe Trotter: 19th-century publisher used Principles of... 121
17 Dr. W.E.B. DuBois: Black America's greatest intellectual 127
18 Dr. Charles Drew: American war hero, patriot, and Blood Bank... 134
19 Ida B. Wells: Exercised Freedom of the Press in 19th Century... 142
20 Dr. Booker T. Washington: HBCU grad, institution builder,... 149
21 George Washington Carver: America's most influential... 156
22 Dr. Daniel Hale Williams: American medical pioneer 167
23 Supreme Justice Thurgood Marshall: Constitutional scholar... 174
24 Dr. Ben Carson: American medical genius, HUD Secretary and... 181
25 Rev. Dr. Martin Luther King, Jr's Mountain Top sermon... 196
26 Dr. Carter G. Woodson: Father of Black History Month 204

II National Parks and Landmarks, Statues, Museums, & Historic Places

27 Places to visit 215
28 Commentary on Patriotism by Major Martin R. Delany 257

29 References   262

About the Author   294

Preface

In 2021, discussions around the 1619 Project and Critical Race Theory (CRT) attempted to re-imagine American history with the false narrative that America is a racist country created to oppress all Black Americans. For example, it proposes the American Revolution was fought so Americans could own slaves and that the Civil War was not a fight to end slavery. My daughter believed those falsehoods and thought that Black Americans "didn't have anything to do with the founding of our country." The more we spoke, I discovered she had very little knowledge about the most notable Black Americans in history. For example, she believed George Washington Carver only invented peanut butter, and Dr. Charles Drew died because they would not let him into the hospital. The entire episode inspired this *Handbook* that began as a series published on the Martin Luther King Republicans' website.

Included are 26 profiles, with photos, of Black Americans whose actions, advice, and advancements contributed to the birth and transformations of our nation. These patriots loved their country and fellow man. They sacrificed their lives, limbs, and reputations to hold America to its founding principles. As a result, they have in common that America has acknowledged them with National Parks and Landmarks, statues, museums, and historical places where future generations can visit and study about them.

All Americans must learn about the patriotic contributions of Black Americans and how our country has honored them. Unfortunately, the 1619 Project and CRT rhetoric portray Black Americans as permanent victims of America, and this *Handbook* is an alternative to that narrative. Instead, the reader will learn that Black patriots like Phillis Wheatley encouraged General Washington to continue in battle, Rev. Frederick Douglass enlisted his sons to fight in the Civil War, and Dr. King's last public speech referenced the 'bill of rights,' as examples of how Black Americans have continued to progress in this country by building on its constitutional frame. I hope that after reading this *Handbook*, you, the reader, will have a better perspective of our country and these great Black American patriots. Many who have been forgotten by time.

Acknowledgement

It is with heartfelt gratitude that I thank the following.

The Most Highest for guiding me.

My parents Dr. Jimmy Tillman and Dorothy Wright Tillman, for gifting me with life.

My children Jimmy III, Jogay, Dorothy, and grandson Joel for inspiring me.

My family DMetra, Ebony, Gimel, Bemaji, Jimalita, their children, and grandchildren for their love.

My President, Dr. Arthur E. Thomas, Central State University (1985-1995), for giving me a chance to learn, to show, and to shine. Also, for including me among the 3,200 students you gathered from across the globe to receive a high-quality education, with high caliber instructors, *to build in deeds, thy greater name.* I hope this book will be placed in the LI-BRARE-REE. For God! For Central! For State!

My friend, historian and educator, Lisa Wyatt. I hope you find this book inspiring so you can write your own. Get well, sis. God is smiling.

My brother James Miller, CSU '95, and Higher Level Productions for feedback and a dope promotional piece and to your beautiful mother, Mrs. Miller.

In memory of Dr. Joseph Lewis and Professor Amos Martin of Central State University History Department. Thank you for your instruction. I wish you were alive to read this work. May God keep you in his heart.

I

Great Black American Patriots

The following profiles were part of the Martin Luther King Republicans 2021 Black History Month Series.

1

Crispus Attucks: American Revolutionary War leader and hero

Crispus Attucks

The Martin Luther King Republicans published the profiles of several distinguished Black Americans and their contributions during 2021 Black History Month. We highlighted those who participated in the founding and growth of our country. Our history in America is complicated, but it is a fact that we have been here since its beginning standing up for faith, family, and freedoms.

CRISPUS ATTUCKS: AMERICAN REVOLUTIONARY WAR LEADER AND HERO

We begin with a tribute to Crispus Attucks. He was the son of an African slave named Prince and an Indian mother named Nancy. Named after the word "attucks" in the Wampanoag language to mean small male deer, he grew to become a stout 6'2 prominent whaler and sea merchant. He was a leader among the seamen, and his sacrifice stirred the consciences of patriots like Samuel Adams and the Sons of Liberty, who use this act of bravery to change the hearts and minds of the citizenry.

This profile is from the *Crispus Attucks Online Museum*, created by the University of Massachusetts History Club. This museum is an invaluable scholarly source for media, historical facts, and in-depth information about Attucks' life and legacy.

Who is Crispus Attucks?

Crispus Attucks has been immortalized as the first casualty of the American Revolutionary War and the first Black American hero. He was in the front line of a group of 50 patriots defying British troops when suddenly shots were fired. Crispus was the first person shot and killed with two bullets in the chest in the historical event known as The Boston Massacre. Four men died, and six were wounded; one man died later from his wounds. As a Black American patriot, Crispus Attucks represents the 5,000 Black American soldiers who fought for an independent America.

As a fugitive slave working as a sailor, Crispus Attucks was always in danger of getting caught. For over twenty years, he sailed out on a whaler from Boston Harbor, and during his time off, he worked as a rope maker near the harbor. In early 1770, competition for work and wages became stiffer as British soldiers competed for the same unskilled positions as locals. This situation created tension which slowly escalated to violent confrontations. On Friday, March 2nd, a group of redcoats and rope makers collided in a bar in Boston. By this time, tensions were high, and on the following Monday, March 5th, on Murray's barracks, a group of rope makers and sailors, lead by Crispus Attucks, confronted a group of soldiers looking for work.

The events of the Boston Massacre started when a young man named Edward Garrick, who had been at King Street insulting the soldier on duty and who had been hit in the ear with a bayonet, encountered Attucks and his group. They gathered twenty to thirty sailors in no time and armed themselves with sticks from the butchers' stalls and cord woodpiles and marched up Cornhill. They made their way to King Street, whistling and carrying their sticks upright over their heads.

According to witnesses' depositions during the Boston Massacre Trial, Crispus Attucks, described as a stout mulatto whose very looks were enough to terrify any person, was at the head of twenty or thirty sailors. Attucks led the angry group, handling a large cordwood stick, and the rest had clubs as weapons. As the soldiers pushed people off, they were verbally provoked and struck with clubs, snowballs as big as a fist, and sticks of any kind. Attucks with one hand held the bayonet of Montgomery and with the other knocked him down. Montgomery immediately fired and killed Attucks. Eight seconds later, a second shot was heard. There were a total of 7 or 8 shots.

Crispus Attucks was the only victim who became known after dying at the massacre. A few days after the massacre, the five men killed were honored in a funeral procession, said to have been attended by 10,000 people. The crowd followed them to the Old Granary Burial Ground on Tremont Street, where they laid their bodies to rest. The Boston Massacre was so crucial to Boston's citizens that patriots observed its anniversary every year leading up to the Independence War.

African hero of the American Revolution

Attucks was celebrated as "the first to defy, the first to die" by poet John Boyle O'Reilly. In 1888, a monument was built on Boston Common commemorating the five men who died in the Boston Massacre: Crispus Attucks, Samuel Gray, James Caldwell, Samuel Maverick, and Patrick Carr. These five men brought a preliminary victory to the American Revolution.

Crispus Attucks continues to be honored by the American public. In 1998, to commemorate the 275th anniversary of his birth, the US Mint issued a silver dollar coin in honor of Attucks. In addition, many schools, children's centers, foundations, and museums are named after him, representing a Black American's struggle and heroism searching for freedom.

TILLMAN'S HANDBOOK OF GREAT BLACK AMERICAN PATRIOTS

Crispus Attucks, the First Martyr of the American Revolution, King now State Street, Boston, March 5th

2

Benjamin Banneker: Colonial Era American genius

Image of Benjamin Banneker. (No portraits of Benjamin Banneker are known to exist. Image resembles an imaginary portrait of Banneker on a 15 cent U.S. postage stamp issued on February 15, 1980

One of my favorite Americans in history is Benjamin Banneker. The legend goes at the age of twenty-one, Benjamin, a free Black American, met Josef Levi, who showed him a pocket watch. Banneker was so fascinated that Levi gave him the timepiece. He studied how it worked, drew a picture of it, and made mathematical calculations for the parts. He worked on building a clock for two years.

In 1753, Banneker completed it. It was made entirely of wood, and he had carved the gears by hand. This woodcraft was the first working clock built in the United States. For more than forty years, the clock struck every hour until it was destroyed in a mysterious fire.

A little-known historical fact was that Banneker petitioned the US government on behalf of those still enslaved. He was a publisher who used the first amendment to write about his faith in God, the importance of family, and freedom for all men. The Martin Luther King Republicans are proud to highlight this patriot and American innovator and encourage all to learn more about Banneker. The *Benjamin Banneker Foundation* in Cantonville, Maryland, is home to the *Benjamin Banneker Historical Park and Museum*, where we gathered the following information.

Who was Benjamin Banneker?

Born on November 9, 1731, outside Baltimore, Maryland, Benjamin Banneker was an extraordinary, self-educated, free Black American. His zest for knowledge led him to become an accomplished mathematician, astronomer, author of six published almanacs, abolitionist, and surveyor of our nation's capital. When Banneker was not stargazing, you could find him maintaining his one hundred acre tobacco farm, orchard, and apiary. Today, his property serves as the Benjamin Banneker Historical Park and Museum location, part of the Baltimore County Department of Recreation and Parks.

His grandmother Molly Welsh provided Benjamin Banneker's early education. She was an English dairymaid who was falsely accused of stealing milk. After demonstrating her ability to read during her trial, Molly was saved from the gallows and instead sentenced to seven years of indentured servitude in the thirteen colonies.

From a young age, Banneker demonstrated an aptitude for math and science. Banneker borrowed a pocket watch in his early twenties and built a wooden clock that kept perfect time for the next fifty years.

In 1772, the Ellicott's, a Quaker family from Pennsylvania, migrated to Maryland and founded Ellicott Mills (now Ellicott City). Banneker befriended this family and eventually borrowed several tools and books on astronomy from them. Finally, he mastered the science of the stars and calculated an ephemeris, a set of astronomical projections for his first almanac.

Impressed by his work, the Ellicott's invited Banneker to help survey the nation's capital. Using the latitude and longitude derived from celestial observations, Banneker was able to lay the base points for the newly established Capitol. Upon his return home, Banneker embarked upon his final project, writing a series of almanacs that included astronomical data and proverbs, mathematical puzzles, and essays on the injustices of slavery.

Banneker published six almanacs between 1792 and 1797. By 1797 his almanacs had become bestsellers. Almanacs, during the eighteenth century, were an essential reference tool used by farmers and navigators. Their collection of astronomical and meteorological data, including phases of the moon, sunrises, sunsets, and weather events, made it easier for farmers to estimate planting and harvesting seasons and navigators to calculate their position on the sea.

Throughout his life, Banneker often questioned the "inhuman captivity" that many Blacks were condemned to endure 'whilst in the chains of slavery.' Motivated by his convictions, Banneker wrote a letter to Secretary of State Thomas Jefferson asking him to recognize the "unjustifiable cruelty" that slavery presented and use his position to seek freedom for those in bondage. Enclosed with his letter, Banneker submitted a manuscript copy of his upcoming 1792 almanac. Jefferson acknowledged Banneker's plea for liberty and forwarded his almanac to the Academy of Sciences in Paris, France, much to the delight of Banneker.

Banneker died in 1806 at the age of 74. He never married nor had children. Following his death, Banneker's reputation as an intellectual man and a respected astronomer and mathematician was solidified by his outstanding accomplishments. For over two centuries, his legacy has inspired many generations to quench their thirst for knowledge and realize their potential to make a difference.

Photo of Benjamin Banneker on is almanac of the year 1795

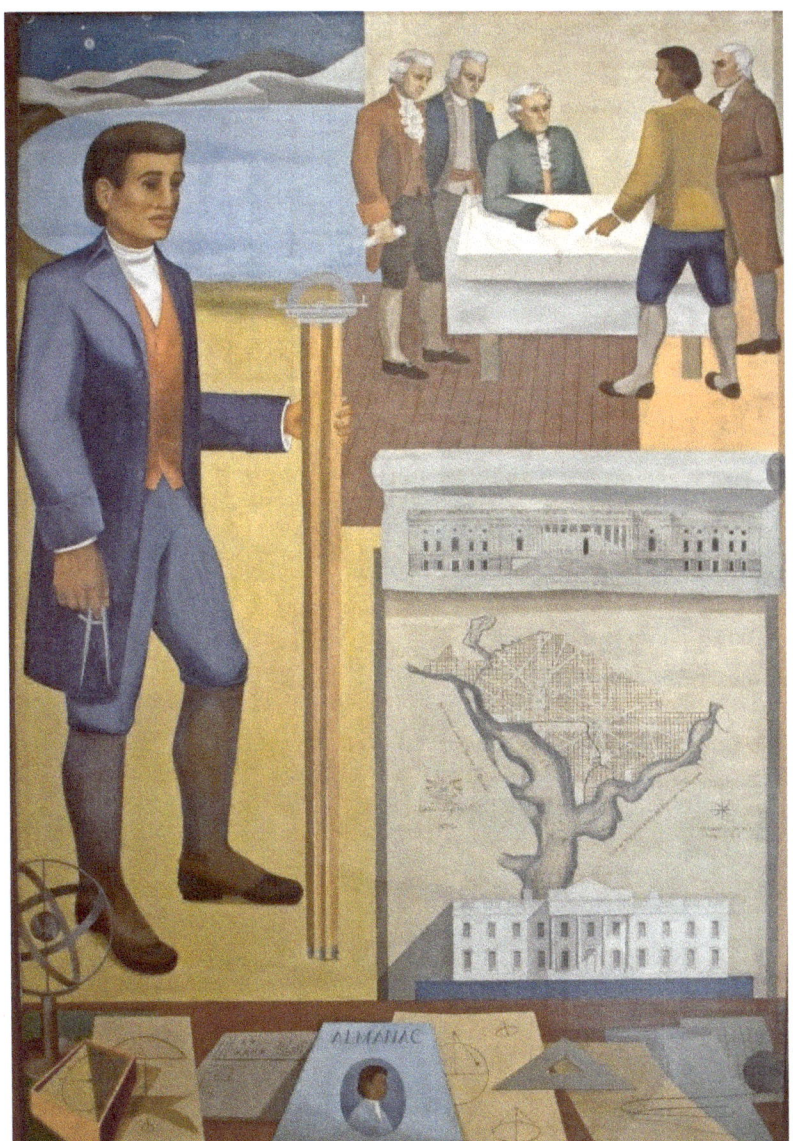

Mural of Benjamin Banneker in the Recorder of Deeds Building in Washington, D.C.

3

James Armistead Lafayette: Washington's top spy that helps win the Revolutionary War

Engraved portrait of James Armistead Lafayette (c. 1759-1830) After the painting by John B. Martin, ca. 1824.

Our country's founding resulted from many acts of bravery by men like James Armistead Lafayette, who believed in the principles of our God-given rights to life, liberty, and the pursuit of happiness. It is estimated that 5,000 to 8,000 Black people participated on the Revolution's Patriot side. For many, their acts of heroism have been lost to a misrepresentation of our history in America. Lafayette was a patriot who risked his life during the Revolutionary and his skills were invaluable to General George Washington.

The Martin Luther King Republicans are proud to celebrate 2021 Black History Month by shining a light on those who contribute to this country even before emancipation and encourage you to visit the Lafayette Memorial located in Brooklyn's Prospect Park in New York City. The following was taken from the *Unsung Heroes Project*, an online source for bios, short videos, and curriculum that preserves and passes on this great history that has been hidden for too long.

Who Was James Armistead Lafayette?

James Armistead Lafayette was a patriot spy during the War for American Independence. He infiltrated Benedict Arnold's forces and provided intelligence that nearly led to Arnold's capture. He also penetrated British commander Lord Cornwallis' camp as a double agent and passed vital intelligence information to General Washington and the Marquis de Lafayette. James Armistead's intel provided the key to the decisive victory at the Battle of Yorktown, which compelled the surrender of Cornwallis and an end to the War for Independence.

A key figure in America's final victory over the British Empire, one could argue that ultimate victory. Therefore, a new nation's birth rested significantly on one Black patriot-James Armistead Lafayette's shoulders. He deserves his place in history where he served next to Revolutionary War heroes General Washington and the Marquis de Lafayette.

James was born around 1748 in New Kent County. During the War for American Independence, his master, William Armistead, was appointed to be one of the managers of Virginia's military supplies in Williamsburg. James Armistead made his way to Richmond and joined the Marquis de Lafayette's service as a patriot spy.

Under the Marquis de Lafayette command, James successfully gained access to Lord Cornwallis' camp and passed himself off as a servant and waiter for the British commander.

It was said in his petition to the Virginia General Assembly that James, *"often at the peril of his life found means to frequent the British Camp, by which means he kept open a channel of the useful communications."*

James Armistead's intel revealed Lafayette Cornwallis' move from Portsmouth to Yorktown. James gave detailed accounts of the British army's fortification of the town and the British forces' vulnerable position.

While in the British camp, James Armistead fooled Cornwallis into acting as a spy for the British against the patriots. He then worked as a double agent feeding the British commander false intelligence about American troop strength and movement. Interestingly, Benedict Arnold, whom Washington regarded as the best military mind on either side of the war, advised Cornwallis to relocate. Had Cornwallis heeded Arnold's advice, the far superior British Army may have avoided defeat. James Armistead's disinformation kept the forces of Cornwallis right where the patriots wanted them.

James Armistead's espionage efforts gave the American and French forces of Washington and Rochambeau enough time to reach the Chesapeake to cut off Cornwallis' retreat, thus directly contributing to American victory and Cornwallis' surrender on October 19, 1781. This last major land battle of the war and meant success for the new American Republic. The groundwork for this final decisive battle hinged on a single Black patriot's efforts - James Armistead Lafayette

After the war, James Armistead returned to Virginia. Because he was a spy and not an enlisted soldier, the Virginia legislature passed a law in 1782 to provide for the freedom of slaves who had served in the war. It was argued that this didn't apply to James Armistead because he didn't serve as "a soldier" only as a spy. In November 1784, the Marquis de Lafayette personally sent a plea for his "honest friend" in a handwritten testimonial for the Virginia General Assembly:

In 1824 the Marquis de Lafayette was invited to America by President Monroe. The Marquis made a tour of all 24 states, including Virginia.

The *Richmond Enquirer* reported that during the event at Yorktown, James Armistead *"was recognized by [the Marquis] in the crowd, called to him by name, and taken into his embrace."*

While the Virginia slave-owners looked on, the famous French general and the Black patriot spy that helped give America its decisive victory stood and embraced one another.

This great American hero, James Armistead Lafayette, died six years later - August 9, 1830.

General George Washington and Lafayette at Valley Forge

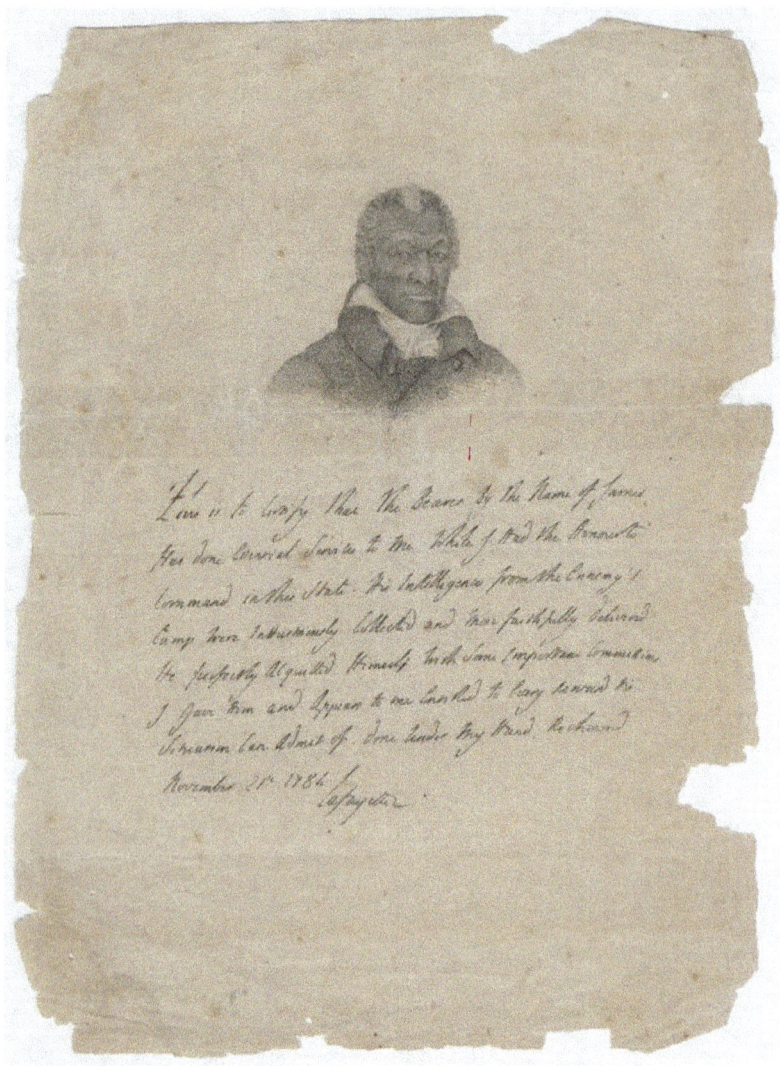

Facsimile of the Marquis de Lafayette's original certificate commending James Armistead Lafayette for his revolutionary war service

4

Phillis Wheatley: Colonial Era influencer

Before there was IG, Facebook, or Twitter, there was a Black American influencer whose thoughts were instrumental in the conversation around the birth of the new nation. Phillis Wheatley, a poet who captured Colonial society's hearts and minds, proved that African slaves had the same intellectual and creative capacity as Europeans. Wheatley commentated on political 'hot topics' like the Stamp Act writing a poem to King George III praising him for its repeal. As a staunch supporter of American Independence, she penned a patriotic ode to General George Washington, who invited her for a private reading at his home.

Wheatly contributed to the literary world and the conciseness of America. She believed in her abilities despite her circumstances because she was of strong faith with access to education. Wheatley inspired future generations of Americans to fight for the abolition of slavery and civil rights.

She had her critics, including Thomas Jefferson and John Hancock, go to court to prove she was the author of her works. It is believed that she penned hundreds of poems, but only fifty-five survived after a house fire. The Martin Luther King Republicans encourage you to visit the Museum of the American Revolution where you can see a copy of Wheatly's *Poems on Various Subjects, Religious and Moral*. A special thanks to the *Phillis Wheatley Historical Society*, created by the University of Massachusetts History Club, for honoring and appreciating Wheatley's contribution to American history and where you can find this information.

Who was Phillis Wheatley?

Although the date and place are not documented, scholars believe that Phillis Wheatley was born in 1753 in West Africa, most likely in present-day Senegal or Gambia. Wheatley was brought to British-ruled Boston, Massachusetts, on July 11, 1761.

At the age of 14, she wrote her first poem, *"To the University of Cambridge, in New England."* Recognizing her literary ability, the Wheatley family supported Phillis' education and relieved her household labor.

By the time she was 18, Wheatley had gathered 28 poems for which she, with the help of Mrs. Wheatley, ran advertisements for subscribers in Boston newspapers in February 1772. When the colonists were unwilling to support literature, she and the Wheatleys turned in frustration to London for a publisher. Wheatley had forwarded the Whitefield poem to Selina Hastings, Countess of Huntingdon, to whom Whitefield had been chaplain. A wealthy supporter of evangelical and abolitionist causes, the countess instructed bookseller Archibald Bell to begin correspondence with Wheatley to prepare the book.

Wheatley, suffering from a chronic asthma condition and Nathaniel, left for London on May 8, 1771. Several dignitaries welcomed the now-celebrated poet: abolitionists' patron the Earl of Dartmouth, poet and activist Baron George Lyttleton, Sir Brook Watson (soon to be the Lord Mayor of London), philanthropist John Thorton, and Benjamin Franklin. While Wheatley was recrossing the Atlantic to reach Mrs. Wheatley, who, at the summer's end, had become seriously ill, Bell was circulating the first edition of *Poems on Various Subjects, Religious and Moral* (1773), the first volume of poetry by a Black American published in modern times.

Poems on Various Subjects revealed that Wheatley's favorite poetic form was the couplet, both iambic pentameter and heroic. More than one-third of her canon is composed of elegies, poems on the deaths of noted persons, friends, or even strangers whose loved ones employed the poet. The verses that best demonstrate her abilities and are often questioned by detractors use classical themes and techniques. In her epyllion "Niobe in Distress for Her Children Slain by Apollo, from Ovid's *Metamorphoses*, Book VI, and from a view of the Painting of Mr.

Richard Wilson," she not only translates Ovid but adds her beautiful lines to extend the dramatic imagery. In *"To Maecenas,"* she transforms Horace's ode into a celebration of Christ.

In addition to classical and neoclassical techniques, Wheatley applied biblical symbolism to evangelize and comment on slavery. For instance, *"On Being Brought from Africa to America,"* the best-known Wheatley poem, chides the Great Awakening audience to remember that believers must include Africans in the Christian stream: *"Remember, Christians, Negroes, black as Cain, /May be refin'd and join th' angelic train."*

The remainder of Wheatley's themes can be classified as celebrations of America. She was strongly influenced by her studies of Alexander Pope, John Milton, the ancient Greek epics of Homer, and the Roman poets Horace and Virgil. She was the first to applaud this nation as glorious *"Columbia"* and that in a letter to no less than the first president of the United States, George Washington, with whom she had corresponded and whom she was later privileged to meet. In 1775, she sent a copy of a poem entitled *"To His Excellency, George Washington."* Washington invited Wheatley to visit his headquarters in Cambridge, Massachusetts, which she did in March 1776. Thomas Paine republished the poem in the Pennsylvania Gazette in April 1776.

Her love of virgin America, as well as her religious fervor, is further suggested by the names of those colonial leaders who signed the attestation that appeared in some copies of *Poems on Various Subjects* to authenticate and support her work: Thomas Hutchinson, governor of Massachusetts; John Hancock; Andrew Oliver, lieutenant governor; James Bowdoin; and Reverend Mather Byles.

Phillis Wheatley, Negro servant to Mr. John Wheatley, of Boston.

Letter from General George Washington to Phillis Wheatley

5

Prince and Primus Hall: Father/Son Colonial Army heroes

Portrait of Prince Hall

PRINCE AND PRIMUS HALL: FATHER/SON COLONIAL ARMY HEROES

There are many unsung heroes among the Black men that served in the early American colonial militias. The father and son duo of Prince and Primus Hall is just one example of the boldness and bravery of Black men who were among those in great Revolutionary War battles like Bunker Hill, Harlem Heights, and Trenton.

They were both free men and patriots who continued their work after the war, associating with the founding fathers. They organized schools and churches, worked as abolitionist and was well respected in Boston. Prince Hall owned real estate, had the right to vote, and General George Washington signed Primus Hall's honorable discharge papers. While their lives were highly notable, we will focus on their patriotic contributions in this essay.

The Martin Luther King Republicans are proud to highlight these American patriots and encourage you to celebrate and study more about the Black soldiers who were a part of our country's foundation. The information in this essay is from various sources throughout the internet, including the *West End Museum* in Boston, Massachusetts. The museum houses an exhibit on both Prince and Primus Hall, and we encourage you to visit.

Who were Prince and Primus Hall?

Prince Hall, Boston's most prominent citizen during the revolutionary period, was the founder of the African Lodge of the Honorable Society of Free and Accepted Masons of Boston, the world's first lodge of Black Freemasonry and the first society in American history devoted to social, political, and economic improvement.

Not much is known of Prince Hall's life before the Revolution. It is written that he was born in 1735 and was the slave of William Hall of Boston. His son, Primus, was born in 1756 to Delia, a servant in another household. In 1762, at the age of 27, the elder Hall joined the Congregational Church, and soon after, married an enslaved woman named Sarah Ritchie. Eight years later, after Sarah's death, he married Flora Gibbs of Gloucester.

A month after the Boston Massacre, William Hall freed Prince; his certificate of manumission read that he was "no longer Reckoned a slave, but [had] always accounted as a free man." Hall made his living as a huckster (peddler), caterer, and leather dresser and was listed as a voter and a taxpayer. He owned a small house and leather workshop in Boston.

Hall and his son Primus were among Massachusetts' six Black men named to have fought at Bunker Hill. A bill elder Hall sent to Colonel Crafts indicates that he crafted five leather drum heads for the Boston Regiment of Artillery in April 1777.

When the American Revolution started in 1776, Primus Hall was 19 when he enlisted in the Fifth Massachusetts Regiment. He would first see war at the Siege of Boston. Primus was a part of Bunker Hill's battle, where many men performed acts of heroism. At this fight, about twice as many British were slain as Americans. The colonists had to retreat because they ran out of ammo. While the British won by technicality, they considered it a hollow victory after counting how many of their soldiers died. After that battle, the colonists pressed against their opponents until the British seized Boston and evacuated the city.

After this victory, his regiment fought at the Battle of Harlem Heights. Commander-in-Chief George Washington led this battle. Here 1,800 American soldiers fought against 5,000 British soldiers and won. A little over a month later, Hall's regiment was a part of the Battle of White Plains.

The next fight would be the famed 'Battle of Trenton', where Washington crossed the Delaware river with more than 2,000 soldiers.

The opposing British army at Trenton was composed almost entirely of Hessian mercenaries. Hessians were German soldiers, "trained from adolescence and continued their training well through adulthood until they were deemed unfit or too old to serve." In Germany, Hessian soldiers were drilled every single day. As a result, they were some of the most renowned fighters in the world.

Despite this, the colonist army (who were almost all commoners) proceeded to attack. The colonists were rewarded with a landslide victory. They captured nearly the entire Hessian force, about 1,000 soldiers. In addition, Primus captured two runaway Hessian soldiers himself after chasing the fleeing soldiers down in the cold for more than half a mile. More than 100 other Hessians were either killed or wounded in the fight. While a handful of Americans were hurt, none died from combat.

A little over a week later, still led by Washington, the Fifth Massachusetts Regiment went to war alongside the British army at the Battle of Princeton—where they were victorious. Primus re-enlisted at the battle of Saratoga and was present for General Burgoyne's surrender.

One of the younger Hall's brothers in combat would write about this battle: *"We had a hard fight. [we] took the British Artillery, but lost our Captain... I was near him [Primus] when Captain Flint was shot through the body... Primus was discharged at the same time with myself.... and [he] was much esteemed by the Officers & men, as a brave & faithful Soldier in the service of his Country."*

After the battle, Washington himself signed Hall's honorable discharge. After the Revolutionary War, he again served his country building fortifications for Castle Island at Boston Harbor during the war in 1812.

TILLMAN'S HANDBOOK OF GREAT BLACK AMERICAN PATRIOTS

Surrender of General Burgoyne

Battle of Trenton

Black soldier on horseback in Revolutionary War

Battle of Harlem Heights

6

Peter Salem and other Black Patriots: Heroes on Bunker Hill

Portrait of Peter Salem

In today's climate, the word 'patriot' is negatively applied as a 'White Supremacist' code word. I challenge this notion, and history has also proven that idea to be false. In the book *Freedom on My Mind: A History of African Americans*, a Black Patriot is defined as a *"Black American who sided with the colonists who opposed British rule during the American Revolutionary War. The term Black Patriot includes, but is not limited to, the 5000 or more Black Americans who fought in the Continental Army during the war."*

The Martin Luther King Republicans encourage you to learn more about Peter Salem and the other patriots whose bravery is often untold. We have listed those noted at Bunker Hill in this essay and encourage you to learn more about them.

This information was gathered from across the internet with a special thank you to the *American Battlefield Trust*. This grassroots organization preserves America's sacred battlefields and educates future generations on what happened and why it matters. We encourage you to visit the battlefields across America to learn more about their precious histories.

Also, for the record, a patriot is someone with the feeling of love, devotion, and sense of attachment to a country and alliance with other citizens who share the same sentiment, and there is nothing wrong with that.

Who was Peter Salem?

On October 1, 1750, Peter Salem was born to a slave mother in Framingham, Province of Massachusetts Bay. He fought in the American Revolution's opening battles at Lexington and Concord as part of the Minutemen under Captain Simon Edgell. During his five years fighting for America's independence, he also served in Captain Drury's company of Colonel John Nixon's 6th Massachusetts Regiment.

Salem was one of the heroes at one of the most significant revolutionary battles, the Battle of Bunker Hill. A British commander, Major John Pitcairn, was shot at least a half dozen times in the war. The final shot was a fatal wound to the head. Peter Salem was one of those who struck the Major, and according to some witnesses, he was the one who delivered the fatal blow.

The moment that Salem shot Pitcairn is immortalized in John Trumbull's famous painting of the Battle of Bunker Hill, that hangs in the Museum of Fine Arts in Boston, Massachusetts. The Daughters of the American Revolution made Salem's home in Leicester a historical monument in 1909, to preserve Salem's memorial and educate the public about his life.

Who was Barzillai Lew?

Barzillai Lew was born free, in Groton, Massachusetts, in 1743, to a "mulatto" slave owned by Captain Samuel Scripture named Margaret Lew. The prominent American Revolutionary War hero was an accomplished musician and served as a musician in the French and Spanish wars. The husband and father, Lew, was called to serve as a fifer, drummer, and soldier in Captain John Ford's Chelmsford Militia in the Battle of Bunker Hill. His Portrait sits in the US State Department Public Room.

Who was Salem Poor?

Salem Poor was sold as an infant at the Salem slave market and brought to Andover by Lydia Abbot. He was baptized in the North Parish Church in 1747. Poor purchased his freedom from John Poor on July 10, 1769, for 27 pounds, a man's annual salary.

He was 22 years old when he marched off to war in Captain Ames' company to Bunker Hill. He was ordered to be a secondary force that would assist in building fortifications. When they arrived, the battle was raging, so they covered the retreating units that had run out of ammunition. Under heavy fire, the British Regular Army killed five and wounded six near him. As Poor helped those injured, he gradually retreated and killed British Army Lt. Col. James Abercrombie with one shot.

Due to Poor's strength and stability at the Battle of Bunker Hill, officers submitted a petition to General George Washington that described his outstanding abilities in battle. In the citation, Poor was hailed as an 'excellent, brave, and gallant soldier'.

Who was Jude Hall?

It is unknown if Jude Hall was born a slave to Philemon Blake of Exeter, New Hampshire. After being sold to a new master, Hall ran away and joined Hind's 3rd New Hampshire Regiment in 1775. The six-foot-tall and powerful soldier nearly died at Bunker Hill when a cannon blast struck nearby. However, he earned the nickname "Old Rock" because of his strength and bravery.

Who was Ceasar Bailey (Dickerson)?

Caesar was born into slavery around 1749 in Deerfield, Massachusetts. He farmed for Nathaniel Dickerson, a Loyalist. Like other slaves, he was given his master's name as his last name. Many slave owners enlisted their slaves into the colonial militia to serve in their place, so he signed up Caesar to take his place in the Deerfield militia. After leaving the Deerfield militia, he joined Colonel William Prescott's regiment during the Battle of Bunker Hill. He changed his last name to Bailey and re-enlisted after being freed around 1778.

Who was Pompey Blackman (Fortune/Freeman)?

Pompey's beginnings are as mysterious as his name. He was thought to have been from Braintree. His date of birth may have been around 1755. He may have been born free. But, on the other hand, he may have gained his freedom. Until 1785, he was known as either Pompey Blackman or Pompey Fortune. After that time, he was identified as Pomp Freeman.

He worked as a tanner's apprentice and, in April 1775, joined Colonel Gerrish's regiment from Concord, Massachusetts. Pompey then transferred to Colonel Loammi Baldwin's regiment. His heroic service in the American Revolution continued until November of 1780. He fought at Lexington and Concord and the Battle of Bunker Hill. He also joined other patriots in Roxbury, blocking the British Army from leaving Boston at Boston Neck, the only land route out of Boston.

Who was Cuff Chambers?

Cuff Chambers was born into slavery around 1738 in Massachusetts to Samuel Blanchard of Andover. He married a woman named Bette in September 1762. At the time of the Revolution and the Battle of Bunker Hill, Samuel Blanchard promised Cuff freedom if he served in the war. After the Battle of Lexington and Concord, he joined the Andover militia as Cuff Blanchard.

His company was known as "eight month's men" because of the length of their service. They marched to Cambridge in May 1775. Cuff was one of at least five Black American men in this company. Cuff's regiment went on to Breed's Hill to build the fortification, and many of these patriots fought on Bunker Hill during the battle. After his freedom, he took his parent's name, Chambers.

Who was Sampson Coburn?

Sampson Coburn was born into slavery on July 19, 1745. He joined the "eight month's service" in Cape Ann, Massachusetts, in May 1775. Coburn may have had previous military experience because he was the highest-ranked Black American who fought at Bunker Hill as a corporal. As part of Colonel William Prescott's regiment, his company fought in the earthen redoubt during the Battle of Bunker Hill. Five days after the battle, he served on the main guard of troops surrounding Boston under Colonel Loammi Baldwin.

The Battle of Bunker Hill

On June 17, 1775, as British redcoats marched up the heights of Bunker Hill outside of Boston, Massachusetts, patriots met them with a hail of musketry from the defenders of the earthen redoubt. The defenders were a motley collection of colonists from various New England colonies. Included in their ranks of 2,400 were approximately 120 Black militiamen.

The Battle of Bunker Hill (which took place on Breed's Hill) was a tremendous morale boost for the patriot cause. First, after being commanded not to fire "until you see the whites of their eyes," the patriots inflicted enormous losses upon the advancing British troops. Then, after being charged three times and running out of ammunition, the patriots have to retreat and give up on the British. Finally, however, the British got a taste of what they were in for, and the patriots realized that they could go toe-to-toe with the most powerful army on the planet.

This encouragement was because of Peter Salem and other Black patriots at Bunker Hill whose stories are untold, including Phillip Abbot, who was killed, Alexander Ames, Isaiah Bayoman, Titus

Coburn, Grant Cooper, Charlestown Eaads, Alexander Eames, Asaba Grosvenor, Blaney Grusha, Cuff Haynes, Cato Howe, Caesar Jahar, Caesar Post, Job Potama, Robin of Sandown, New Hampshire, Seasor of York County, Sampson Talbot, Cato Tufts, and Cuff Whitemore.

Portrait of patriot Barzillai Lew that hangs in the US States Department Public Room

1975 10 cent stamp depicting patriot Salem Poor

The Death of General Warren at the Battle of Bunker Hill

Archive photo of Salem's home site in Leicester, Massachusetts with stone marker circa 1909

7

Richard Allen: Early American Christian pioneer and first AME bishop

Bishop Richard Allen

Independent Christians created one of the first well-known Black churches in America before the American Revolution. Founded around 1758 in Mecklenburg, Virginia, the African Baptist or "Bluestone" Church is just an early example of Black Americans' religious experiences, originating mainly from the revivalistic spirit of the Great Awakening. This movement lasted roughly from 1740 to 1790 and saw the conversion of numerous Blacks to Christianity.

The Great Awaking was the end of the state's establishment of religion, which the movement accomplished through the Act for Establishing Religious Freedom. The cause of religious freedom was championed politically by Thomas Jefferson and James Madison, but it depended on the widespread support of legions of evangelicals, especially Black Christians.

I first learned about the great works of this patriot in Wilberforce, Ohio, when I was a student at Central State University. Along with the neighboring school, Wilberforce University, it was an environment that held to Allen's beliefs to be strong in faith in pursuit of your education. You will read later about Bishop Allen and the early AME church challenges with segregation and success in taking their grievances to the Philadelphia Supreme Court.

Allen used the Constitution. It is the nation's law and has been a tool for all those who believe in freedom. The Martin Luther King Republicans encourage you to study more about why the early Black church is considered one of the foundational and most influential institutions in Black America. The AME church, in particular. A special thank you to the *African American Registry*, a non-profit that provides the most comprehensive online database resource of Black American heritage. Please visit their website where you can find this information.

Who was Bishop Richard Allen?

In 1760, Richard Allen was born in Philadelphia. He was a Black religious leader, founder, and first bishop of the African Methodist Episcopal (AME) Church.

Allen was born a slave in Philadelphia, Pennsylvania. During the

American Revolution, Richard Allen grew up in an era characterized by the advocacy of individual rights, the growth of denominational Christianity, and the inception of the antislavery movement. Around 1768, Allen's owner, a Philadelphia lawyer named Benjamin Chew, sold him, his three siblings, and his parents to Stokely Sturgis, a plantation owner in Delaware. With Sturgis's permission, Allen began to attend Methodist meetings, and around 1777 he was converted to Methodism.

In the second half of the eighteenth century, Methodism increased in Delaware, Pennsylvania, and Maryland. This Christian denomination emphasized a simple set of virtues that included honesty, modesty, and sobriety. Following his conversion in 1780, Sturgis agreed to let Allen hire himself to earn money to purchase his freedom for $2000. In addition to doing manual labor, Allen began to preach at Methodist churches in Delaware and neighboring states. In 1786, Allen paid his last installment to Sturgis and became free.

That same year, Allen accepted an invitation to preach at St. George's Church in Philadelphia, a mixed-race congregation of Methodists. Within a short time, Allen dramatically increased St. George's Black membership, and the building could no longer accommodate the growing community. White elders at St. George rejected Allen's request for a separate place of worship for Black American members. Instead, they chose to construct separated seating within the church by installing a balcony.

In 1787, discouraged by the fact that the Black worshipers who had helped build the balcony would be relegated to sitting there, Allen joined the Rev. Absalom Jones to found the Free African Society, a nondenominational religious association and mutual aid organization. However, Allen's Methodist enthusiasm drove him to leave the Free African Society after two years because of its nondenominational orientation.

Allen's commitment to Methodism also compelled him to stay at St. George's despite the segregated seating arrangement. One Sunday morning in 1792, Jones challenged St. George's segregated seating arrangement by sitting downstairs. In the middle of the opening prayer, two White trustees forced Jones to leave. Allen and other Black members who had been seated in the balcony then walked out of St. George's. Until this incident, few Black Methodists had been receptive to Allen's call to establish an independent Black church. On August 12, 1792, members of the Free African Society founded The African Church of Philadelphia. Because of the Methodists' discriminatory treatment of Blacks, the church was consecrated as part of the Protestant Episcopal Church, and Jones became the denomination's first Black priest.

However, Allen remained faithful to Methodism and used his savings to buy a former blacksmith's shop and transplant it onto a plot of land he had previously purchased in Philadelphia. After renovations, Bethel African Church opened on February 4, 1794, and Allen was ordained its deacon. After Bethel was officially initiated at the 1796 Methodist conference, White Methodist officials attempted to gain control over Allen's church. Still, a Pennsylvania Supreme court ruling in 1807 declared that the Black Methodist congregation owned the property where they worshiped and determined who would preach there.

Following Allen's example, many Black Methodists formed African Methodist Churches in northeastern cities. Because all experienced similar challenges from White Methodists, Allen organized a convention of Black Methodists in 1816 to address their shared problems.

The leaders decided to unite their churches under the African Methodist Episcopal (AME) Church. Accordingly, they gained control over their churches' governance and placed themselves beyond White ecclesiastical jurisdiction. The attendant's elected Allen bishop of the new denomination, a position he held until his death in 1831. The AME Church immediately became a center of Black institutional life. As its leader, Allen created the Bethel Benevolent Society and the African Society for the Education of Youth. He also published articles in Freedom's Journal attacking slavery and organizations such as the American Colonization Society. Because Allen believed enslaved and free Black Americans could be best served through education and religious instruction, he opposed organizations that advocated Black Americans' migration to Africa.

Although the AME Church initiated missionary efforts in such countries as Haiti and Canada during the late 1820s, Allen kept the church focused on elevating Black Americans, especially those in the South. As he said, "We will never separate ourselves voluntarily from the slave population in this country; they are our brethren and we feel there is more virtue in suffering privations with them than fancied advantage for a season." The AME Church increased in the South after the Civil War and today has a membership of more than 1.2 million.

Portrait of Absalom Jones

Bethel- 1st AME Church

8

Harriet Tubman: Presidential advisor and Civil War top spy

Portrait of Harriet Tubman in late 1860s

During Black History Month, Harriet Tubman's legend is often regarded as the 'conductor of the Underground Railroad.' However, many are unaware that she served as a military leader and advisor to President Abraham Lincoln during the Civil War. The Martin Luther King Republicans have reproduced author Alexis Clark *After the Underground Railroad, Harriet Tubman Led a Brazen Civil War Raid,* which was originally published November 2019 for the *History Channel.*

We are proud to highlight that Tubman's choice to be free and to free others went beyond leading runaway slaves using the North Star, but as a brilliant commander-strategist. During the Combahee Ferry Raid, Tubman freed an additional 700 from slavery and was an advisor to the President. Please enjoy this quick read and learn more about this Black patriot who knew she had a choice to 'Be Free or Die'. Also, please visit the one of the many museums or historical site throughout the nation dedicated to Tubman. They are in New Jersey, Maryland, Illinois, and Georgia.

Who was Harriet Tubman?

They called her "Moses" for leading enslaved people in the South to freedom up North. But Harriet Tubman fought the institution of slavery well beyond her role as a conductor for the Underground Railroad. As a soldier and spy for the Union Army during the Civil War, Tubman became the first woman to lead an armed military operation in the United States known as the Combahee Ferry Raid.

By January 1, 1863, when the Emancipation Proclamation went into effect, Tubman had been in South Carolina as a Union Army volunteer. With her family behind in Auburn, New York, she had established herself as a prominent abolitionist in Boston circles. Tubman, at Massachusetts Governor John Andrew's request, had gone to Hilton

Head, South Carolina that had fallen to the Union Army early in the war.

For months, Tubman worked as a laundress, opened a wash house, and served as a nurse until she was given orders to form a spy ring. Tubman had proven herself invaluable at gathering confidential information, creating allies, and avoiding capture as she led the Underground Railroad. Tubman assumed leadership of a secret military mission in South Carolina's low country in her new role.

"First and foremost, her priorities would be to defeat and destroy the system of slavery and in doing so, to definitely defeat the Confederacy," said Brandi Brimmer, a history professor at Spelman College and slavery historian.

Tubman partnered with Colonel James Montgomery, an abolitionist who commanded the Second South Carolina Volunteers, a Black regiment. Together, the two planned a raid along the Combahee River to rescue enslaved people, recruit freedmen into the Union Army, and obliterate some of the region's wealthiest rice plantations.

Montgomery had around 300 men, including 50 from a Rhode Island Regiment and Tubman rounded up eight scouts, who helped her map the area and sent word to enslaved people when the raid would occur.

"She was fearless and she was courageous," said Kate Clifford Larson, historian and author of _Bound for the Promised Land: Harriet Tubman, Portrait of an American Hero_. "She had a sensibility. She could get Black people to trust her and the Union officers knew that they were not trusted by the local people."

Overnight Raids Launch From the River

On June 1, 1863, Tubman and Montgomery, on a federal ship the *John Adams*, led two other gunboats, the *Sentinel* and *Harriet A. Weed*, out of the St. Helena Sound towards the Combahee River. En route, the *Sentinel* ran aground, causing troops from that ship to transfer to the other two boats.

As explained in Catherine Clinton's book, Harriet Tubman: The Road to Freedom, Tubman was illiterate and couldn't write down any intelligence she gathered. So instead, she committed everything to memory, guiding the ships towards strategic points near the shore where fleeing slaves waited. As a result, union forces could destroy the confederate property while leading the steamers away from known torpedoes.

"They needed to take gunboats up the river," said Clinton. "They could have been blown up if they hadn't had her intelligence."

Around 2:30 a.m. on June 2, the vessels *John Adams* and the *Harriet A. Weed* split up along the river to conduct different raids. Tubman led 150 men on the *John Adams* toward the fugitives. Later commenting on the attack, Tubman said once Union forces gave the signal, she saw slaves running everywhere, with women carrying babies, crying children, squealing pigs, chickens, and pots of rice. Rebels tried chasing down the slaves, firing their guns on them. One girl was reportedly killed.

As the escapees ran to the shore, Black troops in rowboats transported them to the ships, but chaos ensued in the process. Tubman, who didn't speak the region's Gullah dialect, reportedly went on deck and sang a popular song from the abolitionist movement that calmed the group down.

More than 700 escaped slavery and made it onto the gunboats. Troops also disembarked near Field's Point, torching plantations, fields, mills, warehouses, and mansions, causing a humiliating defeat for the Confederacy, including losing a pontoon bridge shot to pieces by the gunboats.

The ships docked in Beaufort, South Carolina, where a reporter from the *Wisconsin State Journal* heard what had happened on the Combahee River. He wrote a story without a byline about the "She-Moses" but never mentioned Tubman's name. Instead, he noted that Montgomery's "gallant band of 300 soldiers under the guidance of a Black woman, dashed into the enemies' country, struck a bold and effective blow, destroying millions of dollars worth of commissary store, cotton and lordly dwellings, and striking terror to the heart of the rebellion brought off bear 800 slaves and thousands of dollars worth of property, without losing a man or receiving a scratch."

But Tubman's anonymity came to an end in July 1863 when Franklin Sanborn, the editor of Boston's *Commonwealth* newspaper, picked up the story and named Harriet Tubman, a friend of his, as the heroine.

Despite the mission's success, including recruiting at least 100 freedmen into the Union Army, Tubman was not compensated for her efforts on the Combahee Ferry Raid. She had petitioned the government several times to be paid for her duties as a soldier. "She was denied because she was a woman," says Larson.

"By the time we get to the Emancipation Proclamation, we have Lincoln setting out concrete spaces for Black men and their recognition in military service," said Brimmer. "But there's not really a vision for the work of women who function in the military bearing arms, particularly Black women."

Tubman would eventually get a pension, but only as of the widow of a Black Union soldier, she married after the war, not for her courageous service as a soldier.

TILLMAN'S HANDBOOK OF GREAT BLACK AMERICAN PATRIOTS

Harriet Tubman circa 1860-1880

2nd South Carolina Infantry Regiment raid on rice plantation in Combahee, South Carolina

9

Frederick Douglass: Ambassador, Union army recruiter, U.S. Marshall, and advisor to the president

Portrait of Rev. Frederick Douglass gazing slightly off camera. circa 1879

Fredrick Douglass is often recognized during Black History Month for his outstanding works in abolishing slavery in America. He is regarded as an excellent author and orator. Many are unaware that Douglass was a reverend and confidant to President Abraham Lincoln. He convinced the embattled President to allow Black soldiers to fight for the Union Army, and some scholars have credited that with securing victory for the Union. It has also been rumored that Douglass drafted parts of the Emancipation Proclamation. This patriot was valued in Washington for his skills and intellect and worked under several administrations in various capacities.

Rev. Douglass was a patriot who loved America. He could have remain abroad speaking about American slavery, but he risked his freedom and returned. Douglass put his reputation and even the lives of his family on the line during the Civil War. He believed in the words of the Bible and Constitution and knew that America could be the best nation if men would govern themselves based on these words. The following biography is from *USA Patriotism!*, a website where Douglass is recognized among the Great American Patriots. The Martin Luther King Republicans encourage you to learn more about Rev. Fredrick Douglass and pay a visit to the *Fredrick Douglass National Historic Site* in Cedar Hill, outside of Washington, D.C.

Who was Rev. Frederick Douglass?

From the outbreak of the Civil War until his death, Frederick Douglass (1818 to 1895) was generally recognized as the premier Black American leader and spokesman for his people. Douglass writing was devoted primarily to a heroic image of himself that would inspire in Black Americans the belief that one's color need not be a permanent bar to their achievement of the American dream while reminding

Whites of their obligation as Americans to support free and equal access to that dream for Americans of all races.

The man who became internationally famous as Frederick Douglass was born on Maryland's Eastern Shore in February 1818, the son of Harriet Bailey, a slave, and an unknown White man. Although he recalls witnessing, as a child, the bloody whipping of his Aunt Hester by his master, Douglass says in his autobiographies that his early experience of slavery was characterized less by overt cruelty than by deprivations of food, clothing, and emotional contact with his mother and grandmother.

Sent to Baltimore in 1826 by his master's son-in-law, Thomas Auld, Frederick spent five years as a servant in the home of Thomas Auld's brother, Hugh. At first, Hugh's wife Sophia treated the slave boy with unusual kindness, giving reading lessons to Frederick until her husband forbade them. Rather than accept Hugh Auld's dictates, Frederick took his first rebellious steps toward freedom by teaching himself to read and write.

In 1833, a quarrel between the Auld brothers brought Frederick back to his home in Saint Michaels, Maryland. Tensions between the recalcitrant Black youth and his owner convinced Thomas Auld to hire Frederick out as a farm worker under the supervision of Edward Covey, a local slave breaker.

After six months of unstinting labor, merciless whippings, and repeated humiliations, the desperate sixteen-year-old slave fought back, resisting one of Covey's attempted beatings and intimidating his tormentor sufficiently to prevent future attacks. This dramatic account of his struggle with Covey would become the heroic turning point of his future autobiographies and one of the most celebrated scenes in all of antebellum Black American literature.

In 1836, after a failed attempt to escape from slavery, Frederick was sent back to Baltimore to learn the caulking trade. With the aid of his future spouse, Anna Murray, and masquerading as a free Black merchant sailor, he boarded a northbound train out of Baltimore on September 3, 1838 and arrived in New York City the next day. Before a month had passed, Frederick and Anna were reunited, married, and living in New Bedford, Massachusetts, as Mr. and Mrs. Frederick Douglass, the new last name recommended by a friend in New Bedford's thriving Black American community. Less than three years later, Douglass joined the radical Garrisonian wing of the abolitionist movement as a full-time lecturer.

After years of honing his rhetorical skills on the antislavery platform, Douglass put his life's story into print in 1845. The result, Narrative of the "Life of Frederick Douglass, an American Slave," written by himself, sold more than thirty thousand copies in the first five years of its existence. After a triumphal 21-month lecture tour in England, Ireland, and Scotland, Douglass returned to the United States in 1847, resolved, against the advice of many of his Garrisonian associates, to launch his newspaper, the North Star. Authoring most of the articles and editorials himself, Douglass kept the North Star and its successors, Frederick Douglass's Paper and Frederick Douglass's Monthly, in print from 1847 to 1863.

One of the literary highlights of the newspaper was a novella, "The Heroic Slave," which Douglass wrote in March 1853. Based on an actual slave mutiny, it is regarded as the first work of long fiction in Black American literature.

A rupture of the close relationship between Douglass and Garrison occasioned a period of reflection and reassessment that culminated in Douglass's second autobiography, "My Bondage and My Freedom" (1855). Although he had befriended and advised John Brown in the late 1850s, Douglass declined Brown's invitation to participate in the Harpers Ferry raid but was forced to flee his Rochester, New York, home for Canada in October 1859 after he was publicly linked to

Brown.

Applauding the election of Abraham Lincoln and welcoming the Civil War as a final means of ending slavery, Douglass lobbied the new President in favor of Black American recruitment for the Union Army. When the war ended, Douglass pleaded with President Andrew Johnson for a national voting rights act that would give Black Americans the franchise in all the states.

Douglass's loyalty to the Republican Party, whose candidates he supported throughout his later years, won him an appointment to the highest political offices that any Black American from the North had ever won: federal marshal and recorder of deeds for the District of Columbia, president of the Freedman's Bureau Bank, consul to Haiti, and charge d'affaires for the Dominican Republic.

The income Douglass earned from these positions, coupled with the fees he received for his famous lectures, most notably one entitled "Self-Made Men," and his investments in real estate, allowed Douglass and his family to live in comfort in Uniontown, just outside Washington, D.C. during the last two decades of his life.

His final memoir, "Life and Times of Frederick Douglass," first published in 1881 and expanded in 1892, did not excite the admiration of reviewers or sell widely, as had his first two autobiographies. But the Life and Times maintained Douglass's conviction that he had been a "life of victory, if not complete, at least assured." Life and Times shows Douglass dedicated to the idea of building a racially integrated America, in which skin color would cease to determine an individual's social value and economical options.

In the last months of his life, Douglass decried the increasing incidence of lynching in the South and disputed the notion that a more peaceful social climate would prevail throughout the nation by disenfranchising the Black American man. Yet, Douglass never forsook his long-standing belief that the U.S. Constitution, if strictly and equally enforced, remained the best safeguard for Black American civil and human rights.

In the history of Black American literature, Douglass's importance and influence are immeasurable.

Frederick Douglass embodied three keys for success in life:

- Believe in yourself.
- Take advantage of every opportunity.
- Use the power of spoken and written language to effect positive change for yourself and society.

Douglass said, "What is possible for me is possible for you." By taking these keys and making them his own, Frederick Douglass created a life of honor, respect, and success that he could never have dreamed of when still a boy on Colonel Lloyd's plantation on the Eastern Shore of Maryland.

Did you know?

Douglass believed photography was critical in ending slavery and racism. He thought that the camera would not lie, even in the hands of a racist White, as photographs were an excellent counter to the many racist caricatures, like Blackface. He was the most photographed American of the 19th century, using photography to advance his political views.

Mrs. Anna Murray Douglass's wife for 44 years, portrait ca. 1860

Retouched portrait of Frederick Douglass taken in the 1840s

Rev. Douglass reading at office in Cedar Hill.

TILLMAN'S HANDBOOK OF GREAT BLACK AMERICAN PATRIOTS

Composite of several images of Frederick Douglass the most photographed man of his time.

10

Robert Smalls: Civil War pilot, sea captain & Republican leader in Congress

Captain Robert Smalls

Many have criticized Kanye West's comments about slavery being a 'choice.' This critique fails to recognize the countless Blacks who did not accept their circumstances. Many committed acts of bravery and pressed toward freedom. On May 13, 1862, in the middle of the American Civil War, Robert Smalls freed himself, his crew, and their families from slavery. The fearless Smalls led an uprising aboard a Confederate transport ship, the CSS Planter, located in Charleston harbor, and sailed toward freedom. His feat successfully helped the argument that persuaded President

Abraham Lincoln to accept Black soldiers into the Union Army. After that victory, Smalls continued to travel over America to speak about the daring feat and raise support for the Union.

Robert Smalls was a patriot who became a ship's pilot and sea captain for the Union Army during Civil War. He knew that the fate of thousands of slaves was at issue, as well as the future of the country. After the war, he contributed as a politician, serving in the state senate and then among the first Black Americans elected to the U.S. Congress. As a civil servant, Smalls used his position in the U.S. Customs Office to hire newly freed slaves to demonstrate their abilities to unify the country. Although he faced challenges from Southern Democrats and their army, the Klu Klux Klan, he never wavered in his support for the country. He understood that the Constitution was for all citizens, and he believed in its principles. During this time, his former master's house was up for delinquent taxes, and Smalls purchased the property. This transaction was so controversial that in 1875, it was contested in court. The U.S. Supreme Court ultimately heard the case, and Smalls prevailed. The house remained with his family until 1953.

The Martin Luther King Republicans encourage you to study more about Blacks who did not settle for their enslaved conditions, like Smalls. There is an excellent documentary, *Congressman Robert Smalls: A Patriot's Journey from Slavery to Capitol Hill.* You can also visit Beaufort, South Carolina, to see the *Robert Smalls House* or the *Reconstruction Era National Park*, where the National Park Services curates an exhibit to Smalls and where you can find the information gathered in this essay. We would encourage you to visit the monument dedicated to Smalls in Charleston, but sadly it was vandalized by ANTIFA in 2016.

Who was Robert Smalls?

Robert Smalls was born into slavery in Beaufort, South Carolina. At age twelve, Smalls' master sent him to Charleston to find work. Sending slaves to the city to "hire themselves out" was common in the nineteenth century. Slaves were required to send any money they made home to their masters. Working at a variety of jobs aboard boats, Smalls learned to navigate Charleston Harbor's waterways. At the beginning of the Civil War, Smalls worked as a steersman aboard the *CSS Planter*, a steamboat chartered by the Confederate government to act as a dispatch and survey boat.

On May 12, 1862, he and other enslaved crew members were detailed to load some heavy guns onto the *Planter* to be taken to a Confederate fort. They stretched out the work so that the guns would have to remain aboard overnight. When the White captain, engineer, and mate went into town for the evening, Smalls put on the captain's straw hat and sailed the vessel to another pier where his family and friends waited. They boarded, and he sailed out of Charleston Harbor, blowing the steam whistle at the appropriate checkpoints for safe passage past Forts Sumter and Moultrie.

Then, just out of range of their guns, Smalls raised the white flag of surrender and turned over the *Planter* and all the guns and military supplies aboard to the *USS Onward*, part of the Union blockade fleet. Through his daring act, Smalls secured everyone's freedom on board and instantly became a Union war hero.

Rear Admiral Samuel F. DuPont wrote to Secretary of the Navy Gideon Welles that *"This man, Robert Smalls, is superior to any who has yet come into the lines, intelligent as many of them (contraband slaves) have been. His information has been most interesting, and portions of it of the utmost importance."*

The Southern press was, however, understandably frustrated. The

Charleston Daily Courier reported that *"this vessel (the Planter), which has been allowed to escape under our very noses, to the enemy with a heavy responsibility somewhere, had on board six cannon."*

Recognized for his bravery and skill, Smalls became one of the first Black American pilots in the United States Navy. He was wounded on April 7, 1863, while piloting the *USS Keokuk* during the ironclad attack on Fort Sumter. He also served as a captain for the US Navy during Charleston's siege, 1863-1865.

After the Civil War, Smalls served in various public offices, including the United States House of Representatives. Smalls continued to fight for equality for Black Americans throughout his political career.

Images of Planter's crew adapted from "Heroes in Ebony–The captors of the Rebel steamer Planter, Robert Small, W. Morrison, A. Gradine and John Small

Robert Smalls, captain of the gun-boat "Planter" The gun-boat "Planter," run out of Charleston, S.C., by Robert Smalls, May. South Carolina Charleston, 1862

Rep. Robert Smalls

11

Major Dr. Alexander T. Augusta: Free man and Civil War surgeon

Photo of Major Dr. Alexander Augusta

M any would be surprised to learn that a Black man born in 1825 would become a surgeon, veteran of the American

Civil War, and the first Black professor of medicine in the United States. Major Alexander T. Augusta was a man who lived during a time when there were obstacles, yet he did not let that stop him from pursuing his desire to become a doctor or from serving his country and fellow man during the Civil War. The patriot Augusta was not alone. He is among the 13 known Black Americans that served as surgeons during the American Civil War. He ranked the highest of the two Black commissioned officers in the U.S. Army.

On several occasions, even in military uniform, Augusta experienced discrimination. These incidents were considered the motivation for early anti-discrimination laws. Anti-slavery supporter Senator Charles Sumner was outraged upon hearing that Augusta had to walk in the rain to a court-martial hearing because he was rejected from a streetcar for not giving up his seat. Sumner brought a resolution before the United States Congress to abolish the exclusion of Blacks from railroad privileges in the nation's capital. This action resulted in the desegregation of streetcars in Washington, D.C., within a year.

He was also violently attacked while on a train in Baltimore, Maryland. Several young White men picked out Augusta for wearing his major's uniform. He responded to the incident in a patriotic letter to the weekly Black newspaper, *The Christian Recorder*. He defended his right to wear his uniform out in public. He stated, *"...my position as an officer of the United States, entitles me to wear the insignia of my office, and if I am either afraid or ashamed to wear them, anywhere, I am not fit to hold my commission."*

The Martin Luther King Republicans encourage you to learn more about the attributes of Black Americans like Augusta, who lived in early America, and how they succeeded with much less access as compared to today. For more information on Alexander T. Augusta and Black American surgeons in the Civil War, please visit the *Binding Wounds, Pushing Boundaries: African Americans in Civil War Medicine* exhibition website, where the information in this essay is gathered.

Who was Major Dr. Alexander T. Augusta?

Augusta was born to free African-American parents in Norfolk, Virginia. He began to learn to read while working as a barber, although it was illegal to do so in Virginia. Augusta applied to study medicine at the University of Pennsylvania but was refused admission. Nevertheless, he took private instruction from someone on the faculty. Augusta traveled to California and earned the funds necessary to pursue his goal of becoming a doctor. He enrolled at Trinity College of the University of Toronto in 1850 and conducted business as a druggist and chemist. Six years later, he received a degree in medicine.

Augusta went to Washington, D.C., wrote Abraham Lincoln offering his services as a surgeon, and was given a Presidential commission in the Union Army in October 1862. On April 4, 1863, he received a major's commission as a Black troops surgeon, making him the United States Army's first African-American physician out of eight in the Union Army and its highest-ranking African-American officer at the time. Augusta returned to private practice in Washington, D.C. He was an attending surgeon to the Smallpox Hospital in Washington in 1870. He also served on the local Freedmen's Hospital staff and was placed in charge of the hospital in 1863.

Mustering out of the service in October 1866, this patriot accepted an assignment with the Freedmen's Bureau, heading the agency's Lincoln Hospital in Savannah, Georgia. While there, he encouraged African-American self-help, urged the freedmen to support independent institutions, and gained respect from the city's White physicians.

Augusta taught anatomy in the recently organized medical department at Howard University. He led from November 8, 1868, to July 1877, becoming the first Black American appointed to the school's faculty and any medical college in the U.S. He received honorary degrees of M.D. in 1869 and A.M. in 1871 from Howard in recognition of his contributions.

Several years later, Augusta testified before a Congressional Committee on behalf of his patient Kate Brown, who was seriously injured when she was forcibly ejected from the "White people's car" on a train bound for Washington.

The case went all the way to the Supreme Court; the 1873 Railroad Company v. Brown decision ruled that White and Black passengers must be treated equally using the railroad's cars.

Dr. Alexander T. Augusta died at home four days before Christmas, 1890. Even in death, Augusta broke the color barrier. Interred with full military honors, he became the first Black officer buried at Arlington National Cemetery.

Howard University Medical Faculty. Augusta on left.

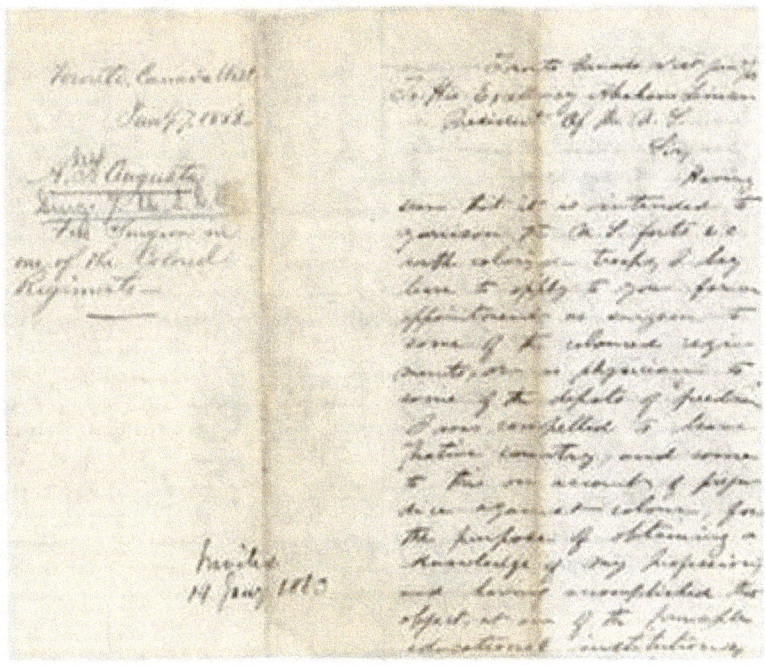

January 7, 1863: Letter from Dr. Augusta to President Lincoln

TILLMAN'S HANDBOOK OF GREAT BLACK AMERICAN PATRIOTS

Freedman's Hospital

Dr. Augusta tombstone at Arlington Cemetery

12

Greenbury Logan: Alamo War hero who fought for Texas Independence

GREENBURY LOGAN: ALAMO WAR HERO WHO FOUGHT FOR TEXAS...

Portrait of Greenbury Logan

'Remember the Alamo!' is a cry known widely in America's history. What is unknown is the many Blacks who participated in Texas's emancipation. At that time, Texas was a territory where Blacks could live freely. Greenbury Logan was a successful businessman who joined hundreds of other Black men who took up arms against Mexico during many battles for independence.

Historian William Katz writes, *"In 1835, when Americans in Texas demanded independence from Mexico, Greenbury Logan was among the Black Texans who agreed to shoulder arms for America. ...when he answered*

Stephen Austin's call for U.S settlers. After meeting with Austin, Logan was granted a quarter-acre plot and Texas citizenship. He came to love the country where he felt himself more a freeman than in the states."

He was not alone. It is reported that a Black man named Joe testified before the signers of the Texas Declaration of Independence about being a survivor of the attack at the Alamo. His testimony provided the information needed to communicate the Texas cabinet's weight as the invading Mexican Army crossed the Texas frontier.

The Martin Luther King Republicans encourage you to study more about these individuals who fought for the Lone Star state and to visit the *Texas African American Monument* in Austin commemorating them, where this profile can be found.

Who was Greenbury Logan?

Greenbury (Greenberry) Logan, a free Black and soldier who fought in the Texas Revolution, was born into slavery about 1798 in Kentucky. He was emancipated by his White father, David Logan, and emigrated from Missouri to Texas in February 1831 to settle in Stephen F. Austin's third colony. Logan was thirty-three years old when he arrived in Texas with his twenty-five-year-old wife, Judah Duncan (ca. 1806–ca. 1832), and their five children.

He obtained a Mexican land grant for a quarter of a land league on Chocolate Bayou on December 22, 1831, in present-day Brazoria County and established himself as a blacksmith. Logan's wife, Judah, and possibly all of their children died shortly after their arrival. In 1832 Logan purchased a slave woman, Caroline Williamson (ca. 1802–ca. 1881), manumitted her, and married her on December 30, 1833, in Brazoria County. It appears the couple had no children since none were listed with them on the 1850 census. Furthermore, a petition filed by Caroline Logan in the 1870s indicated she was

Greenbury Logan's only heir, except for Margaret J. Burgstrom (spelled Bergestone in the 1850 census), the orphan of a Swedish immigrant, whom the Logans adopted.

Logan, along with approximately 400 other free Blacks, who had entered Texas by the mid-1830s, were afforded full citizenship rights by the Mexican government. Mexican law prohibited interracial marriages and made the territory attractive to mixed-race couples who wished to legalize their relationships. Logan sided with the Texas colonists despite his newly-adopted country's egalitarian environment when conflict arose with the Mexican government.

Logan served at the Battle of Velasco on June 26, 1832, and later, in 1835, he answered the call for volunteers to march to Bexar. He joined, in the middle of October, James Walker Fannin's company as a private. This patriot was with a detachment of approximately ninety men from Stephen F. Austin's main force when they defeated a more significant Mexican force near Mission Concepción on October 28, 1835.

At the siege of Bexar, while he served in Captain John York's company, Logan volunteered to storm the works. On December 5, 1835, he was wounded when a ball passed through his right arm on the first day of action. Having "almost entirely lost the use of his right arm," Logan was commended by the Texas legislature, which praised his conduct by declaring he had served "with distinguished alacrity." At thirty-eight, he was discharged from the Army and opened a boarding house, tavern, and retail store in Brazoria with his wife.

On January 5, 1836, the Texas legislature prohibited Blacks from entering the state while granting temporary residency to those already there. Soon after that, the Republic of Texas's new constitution was adopted and prohibited any person of color from residing in the republic without the legislature's consent. On May 15, 1837, Logan petitioned the Texas Congress and stated that he "had hoped that after the zeal and patriotism" he had shown in "fighting for the liberty of his adopted Country," he might be allowed to spend "the remainder of his days in quiet and peace," but understood the constitution would not let him do so without the consent of the legislature. The legislature recommended that Logan and his wife Caroline be "authorized to remain permanently and enjoy all the rights, privileges [sic], and immunities of free Citizens."

In June 1838, Logan received a bounty warrant for 320 acres for his service from October 4, 1835, to December 23, 1835, and a donation certificate for 640 acres for his service during the siege of Bexar. Logan penned a letter to his congressman, Robert Forbes, on November 22, 1841, informing him that he was in every fight during the campaign of 1835 and was the third man that fell when Texan revolutionist took Bexar. Finding himself in an impoverished state, he sought a pension to retain his property in the form of a remission of taxes.

In 1860 Logan, his wife, and their adopted daughter Margaret were listed on the federal census as living in Fort Bend County. He was listed as a blacksmith with real estate valued at $2,500 and a personal estate valued at $3,000. His name was listed on Fort Bend County tax rolls in 1866. According to some genealogy sources, Greenbury Logan passed away about 1868, but his death's exact year is unclear. His widow, Caroline, lived out the remainder of her years with her adopted daughter, Margaret, who married William A. Taylor, in Fort Bend County, Texas, on September 10, 1863. On July 21, 1881, Caroline Logan received her last allotment of land for her husband's service, 1,280 acres, which she sold the following month.

GREENBURY LOGAN: ALAMO WAR HERO WHO FOUGHT FOR TEXAS...

Painting of Greenbury Logan in the Battle of Jacinto

Hendrick Arnold and Greenbury Logan at Siege of Bexar

13

Hendrick Arnold: Leader and spy during Texas Revolution

HENDRICK ARNOLD: LEADER AND SPY DURING TEXAS REVOLUTION

Painting of Hendrick Arnold

Many Blacks participated in the battle for Texas' independence. At that time, Texas was a territory where Blacks could live freely. Hendrick Arnold was an outstanding Black patriot who joined hundreds of other Black men who took up arms against Mexico. He was a brave leader and strategist for the outnumbered Texas colonists. It is reported that the Siege of Bexar was postponed because his company wouldn't march without him. Legend has it that Arnold would hit his drum to sound like rapid gun fire, scaring the Mexican soldiers. Sadly his, and others like Greenbury Logan's, bravery has been lost during Black History Month celebrations. The Martin Luther King Republicans encourage you to study more about these individuals who fought to establish the Lone Star state and visit the *Texas African American Monument* in Austin commemorating them. Also, a special thank you to the *Texas State Historical Association Handbook of Texas* for the profile included.

Who was Hendrick Arnold?

Hendrick Arnold, guide and spy during the Texas Revolution, emigrated from Mississippi with his parents, Daniel Arnold, apparently a White man, and Rachel Arnold. She was seemingly Black in the winter of 1826. The family settled in Stephen F. Austin's colony on the Brazos River. Hendrick is referred to as a Negro, although his brother Holly was regarded as White; both were considered free, although there is no evidence that they were ever formally freed by their father. In July or August of 1827, Hendrick and an Arnold slave named Dolly had a daughter, Harriet. Hendrick held Harriet as a slave.

By 1835, Arnold had settled in San Antonio and married Martina (María), a stepdaughter of Erastus (Deaf) Smith. Arnold had a second daughter, Juanita, who may have been Martina's child. While Arnold and Smith were hunting buffalo in the Little River country north of the present Austin, Mexican forces under General Martín Perfecto de Cos occupied San Antonio. Arnold and Smith came upon Stephen F. Austin's encampment at Salado Creek on their trip home. Arnold, and soon after that, Smith, who considered remaining neutral because of his Mexican wife, offered their services as guides to the Texans. In October, Arnold took part in the battle of Concepción.

When Edward Burleson, who had replaced Austin as commander, called a council of officers on December 3, 1835, the committee decided to postpone an attack on San Antonio, explaining that Arnold was absent and that the officers of one of the divisions refused to march without him. Arnold's whereabouts during his absence are now unknown. When he returned, Benjamin R. Milam called for an attack, subsequently called the siege of Bexar. Arnold served as the guide for Milam's division. Francis W. Johnson, leader of the other division, wrote the official report of the battle for himself and Milam, who was killed during the siege. Johnson acknowledged all the Texan forces' bravery and cited Arnold specifically for his "important service."

On January 3, 1836, Arnold arrived in San Felipe de Austin with his family and Erastus Smith. On January 4, he successfully petitioned the General Council of the provisional government of Texas for relief for their families. He noted Smith's service for Texas and his wounds suffered in battle. Arnold continued to support the revolution and served in Smith's Spy Company in the Battle of San Jacinto.

After the revolution, Arnold was compensated for his service with land a few miles northwest of present Bandera, a relatively unexplored area. Arnold secured adjacent land for his grandmother Catherine Arnold, his father Daniel, and his brother Holly. Holly appears to have been the only family member to settle on the land. Hendrick Arnold lived on the Medina River and operated a gristmill in San Antonio. A portion of the mill was still standing in 1990 near Mission San Juan.

In 1846 Arnold arranged an indentured-servant contract between his daughter Harriet and James Newcomb. Newcomb agreed to pay $750 for her services and then free her after five years. Both Arnold and Newcomb died of cholera before the expiration of the contract. Newcomb's administrator, George M. Martin, petitioned the Texas House of Representatives to permit Harriet to remain in the state as a free woman of color on December 29, 1849. The resolution passed the House; however, Arnold's family made several attempts to regain Harriet from Martin. Martina Arnold took the matter to court, sued Martin for $2,000 plus the $750 due on the indentured-servant contract, and requested that Harriet be returned to her. The case's outcome was cloudy; however, it appears that Harriet was allowed to remain in the state as a free woman. Hendrick Arnold died in the cholera epidemic in Bexar County in 1849 and was buried on the Medina River banks.

Painting of the Siege of Bexar

Painting of Hendrick Arnold and Greenbury Logan and other soldiers moving through the streets during the Siege of Bexar

14

Major Dr. Martin Delany: Civil War strategist, inventor, judge, and writer

Portrait of Major Dr. Martin Delany

Majoring in history at an HBCU can be remarkable. Little did I know when choosing Central State University it would find me in Wilberforce, Ohio, where many great Black intellectuals called home. W.E.B DuBois, Bishop Allen, Charles

Wesley, and Martin Delany were among those men. As students, we would pass Delany's unassuming grave marker (his name misspelled) and share the legend of the 1st Black Major in the Civil War. He provided an essential strategy for President Lincoln and the Union army. Delany even considered emigrating the free slave back to Africa, an opinion held by many Black leaders.

Delany is often forgotten about during Black History Month, yet his accomplishments were so significant. While working along with Rev. Frederick Douglass to publish the North Star, Delany penned what scholars have called "his masterpiece."

In the December 8, 1848 edition, he wrote a lengthy commentary on Patriotism. He writes, *"Patriotism consists not in a mere professed love of country, the place of one's birth – an endearment to the scenery, however delightful and interesting, of such country; nor simply the laws and political policy by which such country is governed; but a pure and unsophisticated interest felt and manifested for man – an impartial love and desire for the promotion and elevation of every member of the body politic, their eligibility to all the rights and privileges of society. This, and other than this, fails to establish the claims of true Patriotism..."* He concludes, "But the time shall yet come, when the name of the despised, neglected American patriot, in spite of American prejudice, shall rise superior to the spirit that would degrade it, and take its place on the records of merit and fame."

That time is now. The Martin Luther King Republicans encourage you to learn more about this patriot Major Delany and have reprinted the entire December 8 article in the conclusion of this handbook. You can also visit his burial site and the *National Afro-American Museum & Cultural Center* in Wilberforce, Ohio, where we gathered the following information.

Who is Martin Delaney?

Martin Robison Delany has been called the "Father of Black Nationalism" because he aggressively promoted Black pride and self-reliance. He was born May 6, 1812, in present-day West Virginia, where it was illegal for him to learn to read and write. Fearing prosecution, his family moved to Pennsylvania, where he could attend school. Then, many years later, he would move his own family to Wilberforce, Ohio, so that his children could obtain a quality education.

Throughout his adult life, Delany was an advocate for Black Americans. He founded and published a Black newspaper, The Mystery, in Pittsburgh and later co-edited The North Star with abolitionist Frederick Douglass. Wanting to provide care to the community, Delany was among the first Black Americans admitted to Harvard University medical school. Before the Civil War, he criticized the government for permitting slavery and abolitionists who lacked commitment to Black equality and justice. Concerned that slavery in America would never end, Delany traveled to Africa to secure a Black American homeland.

With the Civil War outbreak, Delany had renewed hope that all Black Americans would be free. He recruited Black troops for the Union Army and met with President Abraham Lincoln to discuss a war strategy. Lincoln appointed Delany a major, making him the highest-ranking field-grade officer in the U.S. Colored Troops. Following the war, Delany served in the Freedman's Bureau to protect the rights of former slaves.

Delany was an abolitionist, a physician, a leader in Prince Hall Freemasonry, an inventor, a judge, and a prolific writer. In everything he did, Delany was a patriot, determined to achieve freedom and justice for Black Americans. He died January 24, 1885, in Wilberforce and is buried at Massies Creek Cemetery, just two miles from his family home. His final resting place was marked with a small government-issued tombstone—with his name misspelled.

A fund was established to secure a fitting memorial for this remarkable man, not only to honor him but to educate and inspire visitors to the cemetery who may not know that this giant of American history is buried there. The Delany family plot is the resting place of Martin Delany, his wife Catherine, and three of their children, who have no markers. The original grave marker will be preserved in place because of its incredible historical significance. The new monument is made of Black African granite to reflect Delany's pride in his ancestral homeland and features an engraving of Delany as a Major in the Civil War. Bronze plaques provide a summary of his life in addition to the names of the family members buried there.

Military photo of Major Martin Delany

Original grave maker for Major Martin Delany (name misspelled) in Wilberforce, Ohio

15

Dr. Mary McLeod-Bethune: Advisor to the president, civic leader, and patriot

Dr. Mary McLeod Bethune, circa 1910

Mary McLeod-Bethune, the great educator, is usually honored during Black History Month for establishing Bethune-Cookman College and her friendship with First Lady Eleanor Roosevelt. Those things are indeed notable. A little-discussed fact is that she was a Black patriot that laid the foundation for the modern-day civil rights movement. As a presidential advisor, at a crucial time in the country's history, she ensured that the plight of Black Americans' were not overlooked. McLeod-Bethune was the leader of what she called the "Presidential Black Cabinet," led the effort to recruit Black women as officers in the military, and believed in the principles of the United States of America.

Living when Black Americans did not enjoy the freedoms we have today, she remained dignified and made no excuses. She established herself among great leaders and advocated for Black Americans without apology. The Martin Luther King Republicans are proud to share some unknown facts about this great woman and encourage all to visit the *National World War II Museum* in New Orleans, where we gathered this information.

Who was Dr. Mary McLeod Bethune?

Mary McLeod Bethune was a passionate educator and presidential advisor. In her long career in public service, she became one of the earliest Black female activists that helped lay the foundation for the modern civil rights movement.

In his 1956 autobiography, titled *I Wonder as I Wander*, Langston Hughes vividly recalled being invited by Mary Bethune to read at Bethune-Cookman College in 1929. After the event, Bethune hitched a ride with the young poet back to New York City. During Jim Crow, Black travelers were required to carry an Automobile Blue Book that listed the way stops in which Black Americans were allowed to stop for meals, restrooms, or sleeping accommodations. Hughes noted that Bethune avoided much of the indignity of segregated facilities along the long road to New York. He said, *"Colored people along the eastern seaboard spread a feast and opened their homes wherever Mrs. Bethune passed their way." "In fact,"* he continued, *"chickens, sensing that she was coming, went flying off frantically seeking a hiding place. They knew a heaping platter of southern fried chicken would be made in her honor."*

Such popularity followed Bethune through much of her 60 years of public service. During that time, she wore many hats, including educator, community organizer, public policy advisor, public health advocate, advisor to the President of the United States, patriot, mother, grandmother, and great-grandmother. All in the service of her relentless pursuit of what she called "unalienable rights of the citizenship for Black Americans."

Mary McLeod Bethune was born in 1875, number 15 of 17 children of former slaves, during the genesis of Jim Crow and the anti-Black violence that would ultimately plague the South for the duration of her life. By the time of her birth, Patsy and Samuel McLeod owned a small farm near Mayesville, South Carolina. Deeply religious, they encouraged their curious daughter to attend a mission school where she thrived. The young Mary McLeod became so enthralled with learning that she won a scholarship to continue her studies at Scotia Seminary for Negro Girls in Concord, North Carolina, and spent one year at the Moody Bible Institute in Chicago. During her time at Scotia and Moody, she developed her "female uplift" philosophy and her passion for educating girls for leadership in their communities.

In 1898, Mary McLeod married Albertus Bethune and had one son, Albert, in 1899. Her marriage to Albertus was a tumultuous nine years. The family moved from Savannah, Georgia, to Palatka, Florida, where she worked in a small mission school. In 1904, the family moved again to Daytona, Florida, where she founded the Daytona Educational and

Industrial School for Negro Girls. A few short years later, in 1907, her marriage ended when Albertus abandoned the family and returned to South Carolina. Although they never divorced, Bethune listed herself as a widow in the 1910 census. However, her estranged husband did not die until 1918.

In 1923, Bethune successfully negotiated her school's merger in Daytona with the Cookman Institute in Jacksonville, Florida. Together, they created the coeducational four-year Bethune-Cookman College. By the time of the union, she was already a highly respected leader in Black education and Black women's clubs. In addition to her school, Bethune worked with the Florida Federation of Colored Women's Club to found a home for delinquent Black girls in Ocala, Florida. She served as President of the Southeastern Federation of Colored Women's Clubs (1920-25), the National Association of Teachers in Colored Schools (1923-24), and she also served as President of the National Association of Colored Women (1924-1928.) Her work on local, regional, and national boards elevated her status as a Black community leader. By 1935, she founded the National Council of Negro Women, all while serving as President of Bethune-Cookman College.

Her work with the college, national organizations, and her involvement in political advocacy led to President Herbert Hoover's invitation to attend a White House conference in 1930. Bethune capitalized on the invitation and left the meeting a leading advocate and voice for Black Americans in the United States.

During the depths of the Great Depression and the hope of the New Deal, Bethune changed her political party from Republican to Democrat and whole-heartedly committed herself to the betterment of life for Black Americans. In 1931, Bethune was listed tenth on a list of the most outstanding living American women. She used her platform to push an agenda for racial and gender inclusion and championed conventional family life for racial uplift.

Bethune was introduced to the Roosevelts in 1927 and later supported their run for the Presidency. The close friendship with Eleanor Roosevelt was instrumental in gaining regular access to the President. In 1936, President Roosevelt tasked her to join the National Youth Administration, and by 1939 she became the Director of Negro Affairs. As Director, Bethune was the highest-paid Black American in government at the time—with a $5,000 salary. Under her guidance as Director, NYA employed hundreds of thousands of young Black American men and women and established a "Negro College and Graduate Fund" that supported over 4,000 higher education students.

Her work with the Roosevelt administration continued when she established and led the informal "Black Cabinet." The term was coined by Bethune in 1936 and was frequently used to describe President Roosevelt's advisors on issues facing Black communities around the country. The Black Cabinet worked on lynching legislation, attempts to ban poll taxes in the South, welfare, and they worked with New Deal agencies to create jobs for unemployed Black Americans. The cabinet also helped draft the presidential executive orders that ended the exclusion of Black Americans in armed forces and defense industries during World War II. The Black Cabinet's influence grew from Mary McLeod Bethune's unprecedented access to the President and the first lady. The cabinet's work ultimately laid the political foundation of what would become the modern civil rights movement.

During World War II, she mobilized support for the war effort among Black Americans. She publicly argued for equal opportunity in defense-industry manufacturing and the armed forces. In a 1941 speech, she eloquently embodied the sentiment of equality:

> *"Despite the attitude of some employers in refusing to hire Negros to perform needed, skilled services, and despite the denial of the*

same opportunities and courtesies to our youth in the armed forces of our country, we must not fail America and as Americans, we must not let America fail us."

She led war bond drives, blood donation drives and encouraged Black American women to staff the canteens that dotted the country. Bethune also served as a Special Assistant to the Secretary of War for the Women's Army Auxiliary Corps. In the Special Assistant role, she was responsible for establishing a training school and recruiting Black women for army officer training.

Bethune was named honorary General of the Women's Army for National Defense. After the Women's Army, Auxiliary Corps was converted to active duty status in July 1943; she also served as an advisor for the new Women's Army Corps. As an advisor to the WAC and WAND, and successfully lobbied President Roosevelt to end segregation in veteran rehabilitation centers. She frequently briefed the President on violence against Black service members in the South.

Bethune remained a close advisor to the President until his death. She attended his second, third, and fourth inaugurations and delivered a speech in Dallas, Texas, when the news of Roosevelt's death was announced on April 12, 1945. She immediately flew back to Washington and participated in a nationwide radio broadcast celebrating President Roosevelt.

After the war, Bethune served as an associate consultant to the US delegation to help draft the United Nations charter. During the negotiations, she focused her efforts on the rights of people living in colonized countries around the world. She left the conference with a deep sense of disappointment, as she did not get the concessions of freedom, human rights, and self-determination that she so deeply desired.

In 1949, she was invited to Haiti to receive the highest Hattian civilian honor, the "Medal of Honor and Merit." She also traveled to Liberia as a representative of President Truman, where she received the "Commander of the Order of the Star of Africa," Liberia's highest medal. She received 11 honorary degrees from Black and White colleges throughout her life—including Rollins College, where she was the first Black American to receive such an honor in the entire South.

Her legacy continued after her death in May 1955. She was the first Black woman to have a national monument dedicated to her in its capital. Schools, public parks, and streets have been named in her honor. Her most incredible legacy remains Bethune-Cookman University, one of the top 50 historically Black colleges and universities in the country.

Historian Audrey Thomas McCluskey summed it up best when she wrote: *"Despite the numerous instances of racism shown toward her, and even unsubstantiated charges that she was a Communist sympathizer, Bethune maintained her belief in America."* She possessed unwavering patriotism, a strong sense of racial pride and even walked with a cane that had once belonged to her friend, President Franklin Roosevelt. McCluskey continued, *"She lived almost 80 years, a lifetime that reached from the post-Reconstruction era to the dawn of the modern civil rights movement."*

In her last will from 1955, Dr. Bethune wrote:

> *"I leave you hope. The Negro's growth will be great in the years to come. Yesterday our ancestors endured the degradation of slavery, yet they retained their dignity. Today, we direct our strength toward winning a more abundant and secure life. Tomorrow, a new Negro, unhindered by race taboos and shackles, will benefit from more than 330 years of ceaseless struggle. Theirs will be a better world. This I believe with all my heart."*

A little-known fact about Mary McLeod Bethune

President Herbert Hoover invited Bethune to participate in his White House Conference on Child Health and Protection. He appointed her to a commission to plan a "National Memorial Building" in Washington DC *"as a tribute to the Negro's contribution to the achievements of America."* The Memorial was to be *"suitable for meetings of patriotic organizations, public ceremonial events, the exhibition of the art of inventions, and placing statues and tablets."* Congress did not back the project, and private fundraising also failed. The vision finally became a reality more than 80 years later, when the *National Museum of African American History and Culture* opened on the National Mall in 2016.

Mary McLeod Bethune with girls from the Literary and Industrial Training School for Negro Girls in Daytona, circa 1905.

Dr. McLeod-Bethune, circa 1949

Mary McLeod Bethune, Director of NYA Negro Affairs, 1943

Mary McLeod Bethune in WAND uniform, 1944.

16

Monroe Trotter: 19th-century publisher used Principles of Nonviolence to advocate for Black America

Portrait Monroe Trotter

Renowned historian and instructor at Central State University, Dr. Joseph Lewis, introduce me to Monroe Trotter. We examined his work to ensure Black Americans had full equality in all things governmental, political, civil and judicial. Trotter presented petitions, led demonstrations and non-violence protests in the 19th century. A little known fact is that he also a descendant of Jefferson's Sally Hemmings, who gave up his lucrative real estate business to start a newspaper.

Dr. Lewis described Trotter as *"brave enough to speak truth to power"* on his visit to, America's most racist president, Woodrow Wilson to demand adherence to the 14th and 15th Amendments. Those demands made Wilson so mad he had Trotter kicked out.

Trotter was a man who believed in the *matter* of Black lives. When he felt that America did not fulfill the preamble of the Declaration of Independence, he did not want to burn it all down; he tried to hold her to account. The maverick also proved this by not accepting tobacco and liquor advertisements in his newspaper because they negatively affected the community. He suspected the ads were nefariously targeted to Black men.

Like Ida B. Wells, Trotter was a patriot who held up the 1st Amendment and used freedom of the press to inform people throughout the nation. The Martin Luther King Republicans encourage you to study more about Trotter and the Niagara Movement. The following profile is from the *African American Atlas*.

Who was William Monroe Trotter?

Born on April 7, 1872, William Monroe Trotter was a Black news publisher and activist that was called the most militant of the known civil rights activist of the 19th century.

An honor student from Boston, Trotter was the first Black member of Phi Beta Kappa. Between 1897 and 1906, he worked as an insurance and mortgage broker in Boston, Massachusetts. He co-founded the Boston Guardian, a militant newspaper, in 1901, for "propaganda against discrimination." He and his wife Geraldine P. Trotter ran the publication. In 1905, Trotter assisted in founding the Niagara Movement but refused to join the NAACP because he felt it to be too moderate and instead formed the National Equal Rights League.

Trotter caused a stir in 1914 because he strongly protested President Woodrow Wilson's support for the segregation of Black federal employees in the workplace. Trotter came to the White House as a founder and representative of the National Independent Political League, a militant organization that fought for racial and social justice. The publisher of *The Guardian*, a Boston newspaper dedicated to the fight against racial discrimination.

In a meeting with Wilson, Trotter directly challenged the president for permitting the segregation of Black and White government clerks. Angered by this confrontation that questioned his integrity, President Wilson declared himself "offended" and had Trotter removed from the White House. Trotter then took his case to the press and ridiculed the president for introducing segregation into the federal workforce to prevent racial friction. The activist noted that Black and White clerks had worked together without problems for more than 50 years.

In 1919, Trotter appeared at the Paris Peace Conference in an unsuccessful effort to have the organization outlaw racial discrimination. The State Department had denied him a passport to attend, but he had reached France by having himself hired as a cook on a ship. Because of his strident unwillingness to work with established groups, the Civil Rights Movement has been slow to recognize Trotter. But many of his methods were to be adopted in the 1950s, notably his nonviolent protest. He also led demonstrations against events, plays, and films that glorified Ku Klux Klan. William Monroe Trotter died on April 7, 1934, in Boston.

Trotter devoted his career to the fight against racial discrimination and the development of independent political action in the Black community. He led numerous nonviolent protests and demonstrations against conservative Black leaders like Booker T. Washington to accommodate and attack films and plays that glorified the Ku Klux Klan. At that time, Trotter's aggressive tactics were highly controversial, but his activism and approach became a model for the Civil Rights Movement from 1940 to 1970.

The Guardian, A Boston newspaper founded by William Monroe Trotter. This issue is dated August 30, 1902.

Monroe Trotter- founder and editor of The Guardian

17

Dr. W.E.B. DuBois: Black America's greatest intellectual

Dr. W.E.B DuBois

No Black History Month celebration would be complete without a tribute to Black intellectualism and the father of modern-day Black Think Tanks, Dr. W.E.B.DuBois. As a young man, I was a member of the historic Wilberforce #21 lodge, where DuBois was a past member and read some of his writings. His words have been proven timeless.

I am always proud of the accomplishment of men like DuBois, who did not find an excuse or blame others but pressed forward to not only receive an education for himself, but sought to teach others. He did not only study Black Americans' problems; he tried to change a newly emancipated people's trajectory. His idea was the creation of an elite group of educated Black leaders, "The Talented Tenth," who would lead Black Americans in securing equal rights and higher economic standards. My favorite quote of DuBois says, *"A little less complaint and whining, and a little more dogged work and manly striving would do us more credit than a thousand civil rights bills."*

The Martin Luther King Republicans are encouraging you to learn about the people who did not wait for legislation, desegregation, or corporations to address the problems Black America faced. The *W.E.B.Dubois National Historic Site*, in Great Barrington, Massachusetts, is an excellent place to learn more about this patriot and where this profile is located.

Who was Dr. W.E.B DuBois?

William Edward Burghardt DuBois's story begins on his birthday—February 23, 1868—in the small rural town of Great Barrington, Massachusetts. The life and values of rural New England and its small Black American community, some of whose members fought in the famous all-Black 54th Massachusetts Volunteer Infantry Regiment, shaped DuBois's early years and his ideas about democracy, education, and family.

In 1885, DuBois left home for Fisk University, studied in Berlin, and became the first Black American to graduate with a Ph.D. from Harvard University in 1895.

By age thirty-five, DuBois had published *The Suppression of the African Slave Trade*, *The Philadelphia Negro*, and *The Souls of Black*

Folk, his seminal work. He was a founder and leader of the Niagara Movement, the National Association for the Advancement of Colored People (NAACP), and the Pan-African Congresses. DuBois served as the editor of *The Crisis* magazine for twenty-four years and lectured throughout the world well into later life.

DuBois's vision was of a world without human exploitation and equality for all. He understood that the struggle for the equality of Black Americans was part of a larger struggle for freedom and equality for all people. His prominence and ideas were threatening to some. In the 1950s, during the McCarthy era, he was falsely accused of being an agent of a foreign power and later acquitted of all charges.

At the invitation of President Nkrumah, DuBois moved to Ghana at the age of ninety-three to undertake writing the *Encyclopedia Africana.* DuBois's Promethean life ended on August 28, 1963, in Accra, Ghana, where he was honored with a state funeral. His passing occurred on the eve of the historic Civil Rights March on Washington, at which Roy Wilkins, leader of the NAACP, proclaimed to the 250,000 people gathered at the Lincoln Memorial, *"At the dawn of the 20th century his was the voice that was calling to you to gather here today in this cause."*

Niagara movement: meeting in Fort Erie, Canada, 1905. Top row (left to right): H. A. Thompson, Alonzo F. Herndon, John Hope, James R. L. Diggs (?). Second row (left to right): Frederick McGhee, Norris B. Herndon (boy), J. Max Barber, W. E. B. DuBois, Robert Bonner. Bottom row (left to right): Henry L. Bailey, Clement G. Morgan, W. H. H. Hart, B. S. Smith

DuBois at Harvard graduation (seated far right)

Dr. DuBois between 1930-1940

18

Dr. Charles Drew: American war hero, patriot, and Blood Bank founder

Dr. Charles Drew courtesy of the Moorland-Spingarn Research Center.

The 'Big Lie' perpetrated every Black History Month is that the world-renowned and well-respected Dr. Charles Drew died because he was denied a blood transfusion in a 'White's Only' hospital. School children are being taught this misinformation.

This rumor has been used to stoke racial division and reinforces the false narrative that America's race relations have not advanced in 400 years. Spencie Love writes in her book <u>One Blood: The Death and Resurrection of Charles R. Drew,</u>

> "On April 1, 1950, Drew traveled to the Andrew Memorial Clinic in Tuskegee, Alabama, to deliver a lecture. He was accompanied by three of his resident physicians from Howard University. All four passengers were Black. Drew apparently fell asleep while driving. The car ran off the road (N.C. 49 near Haw River) and rolled over. He was thrown out of the vehicle, and the car rolled over him. Drew suffered a nearly severed leg, massive chest injuries, a broken neck, brain damage, and complete blockage of the blood flow to his heart. Only one other person was seriously injured, John Ford, but he eventually recovered.
>
> Paramedics took Drew and Ford to Alamance General Hospital, a facilities-poor "White" hospital. The White doctors at Alamance began work immediately on the two injured men. Drew's injuries were so severe and his blood loss so great that he could not be saved. His family later wrote letters to the attending physicians thanking them for their efforts. Ford was treated at Alamance for several days before being transported to Washington, a Black hospital."

Dr. Drew was an internationally known surgeon who revealed the bond we all had in common, plasma. The medical community appreciated his discoveries, and his techniques are still in use today. This patriot is credited with saving thousands of lives during World War II with the first bloodmobiles and other lifesaving practices.

During the early 20th Century, Black Americans knew they were building on the advances created by those that came before them.

They were the children born after slavery and could measure the progress first-hand. They also believed that God was a part of America's progress. Dr. Drew was not an outstanding student. He was just dedicated. We must not forget these things and continue to move forward with the same dedication. The Martin Luther King Republicans encourage you to learn more about Dr. Drew and visit the *Charles Drew House* in Arlington, Virginia, to find this profile.

Who was Dr. Charles Drew?

Dr. Charles Drew, who pioneered blood banking during the 1920s to 1940s, lived in a modest two-story frame house in North Arlington. He was also the first Black American to receive a Doctorate of Science in Medicine. As Chief of Surgery at Freedmen's Hospital (now Howard University Hospital), Drew passed on crucial training to a new generation of Black surgeons, many of whom would continue to integrate hospital workforces throughout the nation. He also opposed the American Red Cross policy of segregated blood banks. Located just outside of Washington, DC, the Drew family home in Arlington, Virginia, was the physician's home base during his formative years of study from 1920 to 1939.

Drew was born at Freedmen's Hospital in 1904 to educated, middle-class parents. In response to strict segregation laws and social practices, Black Washingtonians had developed strong cultural and intellectual centers. In his early years in DC, Drew took advantage of the institutions created by Blacks, including hikes and picnics organized by the Twelfth Street YMCA. He also attended Paul Laurence Dunbar High School, a nationally recognized Black high school. He had developed high self-confidence and determination.

Drew spent 18 years training to become a surgeon. After graduating from high school in 1922, Drew continued onto college. He began at Amherst College in Massachusetts. Even in the north, Drew experienced institutionalized racism. He could not become the captain of the football team because of his skin color.

After graduating in 1926, Drew briefly taught biology and chemistry at Morgan State College in Baltimore, MD. Two years later, he moved to Canada to attend McGill Medical School. Here he first learned about blood transfusions as a way to treat patients in shock. Drew graduated from McGill and began to teach at Howard University in 1935. Yet three years later, he relocated to Columbia University in 1938 to earn his doctorate. While in New York, Drew met and married his wife, Lenore Robbins. They had four children together.

At Columbia, Drew chose to specialize in blood plasma and transfusions. Along with another student, he developed an experimental blood bank. This project became the basis of his dissertation, titled "Banked Blood: A Study in Blood Preservation." Throughout his education, Drew received scholarships, without which he could not have paid his McGill tuition.

In 1940, Drew completed his Ph.D. and returned to Freedmen's Hospital as a certified surgeon. He wished to settle down after his years of constant transition. However, the outbreak of World War II changed his plans. In September 1940, he moved back to New York to direct the Blood for Britain project. Already engaged in warfare, Britain needed portable blood. The initiative successfully delivered usable blood to those in need of emergency transfusions. In early 1941, Drew became the assistant director of the first American Red Cross blood bank. In April, now a certified diplomat of the American Board of Surgery, Drew returned to Freedmen's Hospital as Head of Surgery.

In October 1941, the Red Cross announced it would not take blood from Black donors. In theory, Drew could not donate blood to the very program that he helped form. Amidst protests from the NAACP, the Red Cross amended its policy. Instead, it would segregate Black and White blood banks. Drew voiced his disapproval of the policy in letters to friends, family, and officials. He argued there was no scientific evidence proving a difference in Black and White blood. In 1943, Drew publicly spoke out against blood segregation. The American Red Cross did not change its policies until 1950.

Until his death in 1950, Drew called for medical schools to end their exclusion of Black students. At his institution, Drew transformed the surgical department and training program. He provided modernized medical services to Black citizens. On April 1, 1950, Drew died in a car accident on his way to a medical conference in Tuskegee, Alabama. Hundreds attended his funeral in Washington, DC. His family buried him in Lincoln Cemetery in Maryland.

The Drew House in Arlington, VA, serves as a reminder of Dr. Charles Drew's years of continuous training and work and his extraordinary accomplishments in medicine and civil rights. It is a monument to Drew's achievements in education and science. Drew's foundational research on plasma and blood banking helped modernize medicine and saved thousands of lives during World War II and later conflicts.

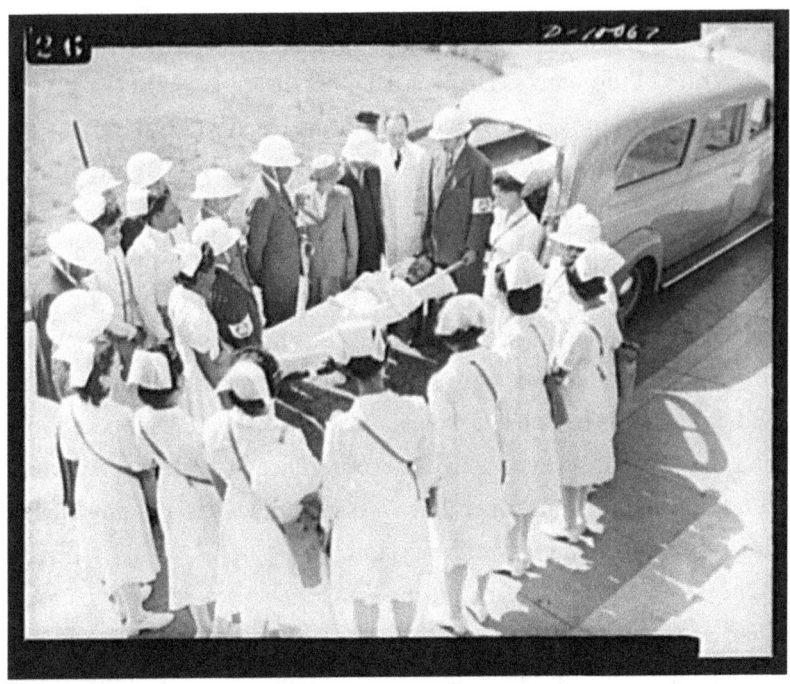

Office of Civilian Defense worker help protect nation's capital. Demonstrating treatment of air-raid victim, medical corps officers instruct nurses in practice raid in Washington, D.C. This photo shows the Howard University medical unit headed by Dr. Charles Drew, which has been rated one of the country's finest. United States Washington D.C. District of Columbia Washington D.C, 1943.

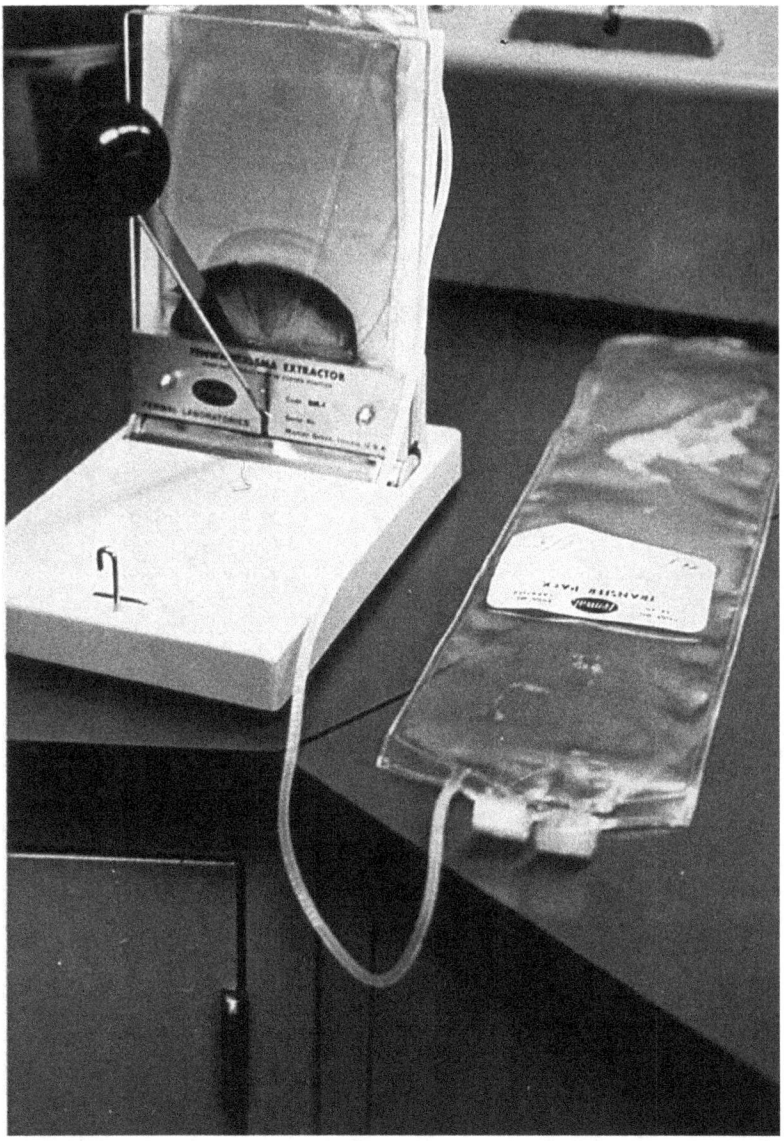
Plasma transfusion package and extractor used to collect plasma from donors

19

Ida B. Wells: Exercised Freedom of the Press in 19th Century crusade

IDA B. WELLS: EXERCISED FREEDOM OF THE PRESS IN 19TH CENTURY...

When I grew up on the Southside of Chicago, very close to the massive Wells housing developments, you came to know the name 'Ida B.' synonymous with "don't take no mess." It was a tough place yet filled with a sense of community pride. In its beginnings, it was a beautiful place that provided housing and supportive services for Black families and was a place for organizing.

These attributes are certainly in the spirit of a great woman who did not allow unjust circumstances to happen to herself or others without a fight.

She was a patriot who understood the first amendment as a fundamental right that Americans have. Wells recognized the value of a free press and the newspaper she wrote for, edited, and co-owned was called *The Memphis Free Speech*. As a writer, Wells was protected by the first amendment to tell the stories and bring attention to Black Americans and their condition. A little known fact is that from 1913 to 1916 Wells served as a probation officer of the Chicago municipal court to assist ex-offenders and monitor local police.

The Martin Luther King Republicans encourage you to study how Black Americans like Wells have used the Constitution and why it is essential to maintain. Also, visit the *Ida B. Wells-Barnett Museum* that is located at the Spires Bolling House in Holly Springs, Mississippi. The following biography is was written by Arlisha R. Norwood, a *National Women History Museum* Fellow and gathered from its website.

Who was Ida B. Wells?

Ida B. Wells-Barnett was a prominent journalist, activist, and researcher, in the late 19th and early 20th centuries. In her lifetime, she battled sexism, racism, and violence. As a skilled writer, Wells-Barnett also used her skills as a journalist to shed light on the conditions of African Americans throughout the South.

Ida Bell Wells was born in Holly Springs, Mississippi on July 16th, 1862. She was born into slavery during the Civil War. Once the war ended Wells-Barnett's parents became politically active in Reconstruction Era politics. Her parents instilled into her the importance of education. Wells-Barnett enrolled at Rust College but was expelled when she started a dispute with the university president.

In 1878, Wells-Barnett went to visit her grandmother. While she was there Wells-Barnett was informed that a yellow fever epidemic had hit her hometown. The disease took both of Wells-Barnett's parents and her infant brother. Left to raise her brothers and sister, she took a job as a teacher so that she could keep the family together. Eventually, Wells-Barnett moved her siblings to Memphis, Tennessee. There she continued to work as an educator.

In 1884, Wells-Barnett filed a lawsuit against a train car company in Memphis for unfair treatment. She had been thrown off a first-class train, despite having a ticket. Although she won the case on the local level, the ruling was eventually overturned in federal court. After the lynching of one of her friends, Wells-Barnett turned her attention to white mob violence. She became skeptical about the reasons black men were lynched and set out to investigate several cases. She published her findings in a pamphlet and wrote several columns in local newspapers. Her expose about an 1892 lynching enraged locals, who burned her press and drove her from Memphis. After a few months, the threats became so bad she was forced to move to Chicago, Illinois.

In 1893, Wells-Barnett, joined other African American leaders in calling for the boycott of the World's Columbian Exposition. The boycotters accused the exposition committee of locking out African Americans and negatively portraying the black community. In 1895, Wells-Barnett married famed African American lawyer Ferdinand Barnett. Together, the couple had four children. Throughout her career Wells-Barnett, balanced motherhood with her activism.

Wells-Barnett traveled internationally, shedding light on lynching to foreign audiences. Abroad, she openly confronted white women in the suffrage movement who ignored lynching. Because of her stance, she was often ridiculed and ostracized by women's suffrage organizations in the United States. Nevertheless, Wells-Barnett remained active the women's rights movement. She was a founder of the National Association of Colored Women's Club which was created to address issues dealing with civil rights and women's suffrage. Although she was in Niagara Falls for [the meeting of the Niagara Movement that led to] the the founding of the National Association for the Advancement of Colored People (NAACP), her name is not mentioned as an official founder. Late in her career Wells-Barnett focused on urban reform in the growing city of Chicago. She died on March 25th, 1931.

Ida B. Wells, circa 1893

Ida B. Wells-Barnett with her children Charles, Herman, Ida, and Alfreda, 1909

Ida B. Wells-Barnett (1862–1931), wearing "Martyred Negro Soldiers" button, between 1917–1919

20

Dr. Booker T. Washington: HBCU grad, institution builder, presidential advisor, and cabinet nominee

Dr. Booker T. Washington

Booker T. Washington has been a subject of scholars as they compare his conservative philosophy to DuBois's liberal one. Even during his lifetime, he faced Monroe Trotter and others' criticism. Yet, these great thinkers had the same plan—to move Black Americans forward. While Washington believed in hard work to education, his contemporaries believed in education to hard work. Both were correct, and in concert, we did move forward. These former slaves and children of slaves knew that their actions would move generations to come. The common thread has been education. Whether from a traditional Ivy League school like Harvard or an HBCU Ivy League school like Hampton, they knew it would be essential to our advancement.

Historically Black Colleges and Universities have been the bedrock for Blacks' advancement in America. These institutions existed during slavery and were a beacon of hope for the runaway. Wilberforce, Ohio, was one of the last stops on the Underground Railroad where Wilberforce University stood to prepare the fugitive for life as a free and educated person.

Booker T. Washington walked from his home to Hampton University in search of an education, and once he got it, he began to teach. Teaching was not enough. He built Tuskegee Institute and, with the president of Sears's help, thousands of other schools throughout the nation.

At Central State University, students were privileged to get firsthand information about Booker T. Washington from his granddaughter Mrs. Edith Washington Johnson, the Director of Financial Aid and Admissions. Mrs. Johnson would be a guest lecturer in Dr. Joseph Lewis' history classes and discussed Washington's strong beliefs about the importance of Blacks using their education to move the race forward.

The Martin Luther King Republicans would like to acknowledge

President Donald J. Trump as a champion for HBCUs. When HBCUs were in serious financial trouble, the Administration worked with legislators Senator Tim Scott, Senator Lamar Alexander, and Rep. Mark Walker because of an impending end to Title III Part F funding. As a result, developed a compromise bill fully supported and pushed by President Trump. This action not only saved that funding line, but it was the first time HBCUs received $255M in permanent funding through the FUTURE Act.

During his administration, Trump met with over 80 HBCU leaders at the White House, moved the White House HBCU Initiative office back into the White House, and relaunched the HBCU Capital Finance Board to make $500 million available to support HBCUs. Trump signed legislation to increase federal funding for HBCUs by 13% and was the first sitting President to speak at the HBCU Week Conference, where he announced America would end discriminatory restrictions to prevent faith-based HBCUs from accessing federal support.

We encourage you to join us in supporting HBCUs with endowments, scholarships, and as ambassadors for recruitment. The following profile can be found in *The African American Desk Reference*.

Who was Booker T. Washington?

Booker T. Washington was born a slave on a plantation in Hale's Ford, in Franklin County, VA, on April 5, 1856. After emancipation, his family was so poor that he worked in salt furnaces and coal mines at age nine. An intelligent and curious child, Washington yearned for an education and was frustrated when he could not receive good schooling. Finally, when he was 16, his parents allowed him to quit work to go to school. Unfortunately, they had no money to help him, so he walked 200 miles to attend the Hampton Institute in Virginia. He paid his tuition and board there by working as a janitor.

Committing himself to the idea that education would raise him and his people to equality in America, Washington became a teacher. He first taught in his hometown and then at the Hampton Institute, and then in 1881, he became the first leader of Tuskegee Institute in Alabama. As head of the Institute, Washington frequently traveled to raise funds from both Blacks and Whites. He soon became a well-known speaker. In 1895, Washington was asked to speak at the Cotton States Exposition opening, a first-time honor for a Black American. His Atlanta Compromise speech explained his central thesis that Blacks could secure their constitutional rights through their own economic and moral advancement rather than through legal and political changes.

Although his pacifying stand angered some Blacks who feared it would encourage the opponents of equal rights, Whites approved his views. Thus his significant achievement was to win over diverse elements among southern Whites, without whose support the programs he foresaw and brought into being would have been impossible. In addition to Tuskegee Institute, Washington instituted various rural extension programs, built over 5000 schools throughout the country, and helped establish the National Negro Business League. Shortly after President McKinley's election in 1896, a movement was set in motion that urged that Washington be named a cabinet post. Still, he withdrew his name from consideration, preferring to work outside the political arena.

In 1901, Washington wrote his autobiography, "Up From Slavery." As a patriot, he was a chief Black advisor to Presidents Theodore Roosevelt and William Howard Taft. Still, he faced growing Black and White liberal opposition in the Niagara Movement and the NAACP, demanding civil rights for Blacks and encouraging protest in response to White aggression such as lynching, disfranchisement, and segregation laws.

Booker T. Washington, who urged Blacks to gain equality through education and economic advancement, died on November 14, 1915.

American educator, economist, and industrialist Booker T Washington (1856 - 1915), speaks to a large crowd during his last pilgrimage in Louisiana, during one of his southern educational tours, circa 1915.

Booker T. Washington, half-length portrait, seated at desk. [Between 1890 and 1910]

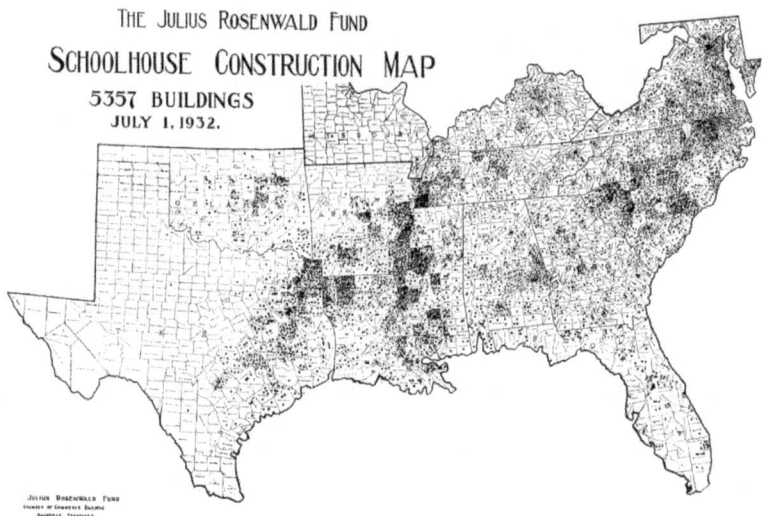

Rosenwald Fund Map of schools throughout Southern state. By 1928, 1 in every 5 schools for Black students in America was a Rosenwald School.

21

George Washington Carver: America's most influential scientific mind of the 20th Century

Every Black History Month, we are reminded of the original Mr. Peanut, George Washington Carver, and his contributions to agriculture science. This quiet, intelligent innovator did not allow the limitations of being a Black man, post-Civil War, to stop him from completing his education and using it to help others. Carver was quoted as saying, *"No individual has any right*

to come into the world and go out of it without leaving something behind." Carver did not profit from many of his products. He freely gave his discoveries to the world. Carver would not patent them or even keep a list of them. He believed that life was to be lived as an expression of God's goodness.

Many are unaware of the times that Carver's scientific mind came to the country's aid. During wartime he provided an alternative to rubber and he assisted in replenishing the land after the deadly Dustbowl. This patriot did not live or die a wealthy man, but one respected worldwide. This chapter will share some little-known relationships between Carver and some of the most influential figures in America.

The Martin Luther King Republican encourages you to visit the *George Washington Carver National Monument* in Diamond, Missouri, to learn more about this genius. Sarah Bolton's Lives of Poor Boys Who Became Famous and Arna Bontemps's The Story of Geroge Washington Carver are two excellent books, along with Barbara Maranzani's 2019 article is where information in this profile can be found. Portions were edited in regards to the relationship with Booker T. Washington.

Who was George Washington Carver?

Carver was born near Diamond, Missouri. He left home when he was about ten and eventually settled in Minneapolis and Kansas, where he worked his way through high school. Following his graduation from Iowa State College of Agriculture and Mechanic Arts (now Iowa State University), Carver joined the college faculty and continued his studies, specializing in bacteriological laboratory work in systematic botany.

In 1896, he became director of the Department of Agricultural Research at Tuskegee Normal and Industrial Institute (now Tuskegee

University). Carver began an exhaustive series of experiments with peanuts, developing several hundred industrial uses for them and sweet potatoes and soybeans. His discoveries convinced southern farmers to raise other crops in addition to cotton. He also taught methods of soil improvement.

In 1935, he was appointed collaborator in the Division of Plant Mycology and Disease Survey of the Bureau of Plant Industry of the U.S. Department of Agriculture. George Washington Carver died at Tuskegee on January 5, 1943.

Carver's relationships

Booker T. Washington helped launch Carver's career.

Carver was a professor and recent graduate student at what is now Iowa State University when he first came to Booker T. Washington's attention in 1896. Born into slavery as Carver had been, Washington was the most famous Black man in America. He had founded the all-Black Tuskegee Normal and Industrial Institute in Alabama some 15 years earlier. So he lured Carver to Alabama to head up Tuskegee's recently-created agricultural department, where Carver would spend the next four decades.

Washington came into conflict with other Black leaders, particularly W.E.B. DuBois, for his conservative, pragmatic approach to civil rights issues. [Washington advocated that Black Americans should gain vocational skills to increase their prosperity, even if it meant accepting racial segregation, discrimination, and a lack of traditional academic achievement].

Carver aligned himself with Washington's thinking, but this didn't prevent the two from clashing. Although his salary was double that of some other Tuskegee staffers, Carver balked at handling many of his day-to-day teaching and administrative responsibilities.

The two were temperamental opposites: Washington, a fastidious, buttoned-up, organized "doer," and Carver, a messy, haphazardly-dressed dreamer, perpetually absorbed by his endless research experiments. Despite these differences, Washington recognized Carver's brilliance and steadfastly supported him over the objections of others. Carver was reportedly devastated by Washington's death in 1915.

Carver became an advisor to presidents and the U.S. government.
Carver first came to President Theodore Roosevelt's attention thanks to his association with Washington, an advisor to Roosevelt on race relations, and once dined at the White House as Roosevelt's guest. Roosevelt first visited Tuskegee in 1905, and Carver was tasked with mounting a presentation showcasing the Institute's work.

Carver continued to advise Roosevelt after Washington's death and until Roosevelt's end in 1919. During his time as vice president, Calvin Coolidge also visited Tuskegee to seek Carver's agricultural advice.

Carver's public profile began to rise in the 1920s, thanks to his pioneering work with peanuts. He appeared before the U.S. Congress in 1921 on behalf of a peanut farmer's lobbying group, where he impressed lawmakers with his knowledge and expertise. Increasingly known as the "peanut man," Carver became a source of advice for fellow scientists and government officials alike.

Thanks in part to an old connection, Carver's influence grew during President Franklin D. Roosevelt's administration. Carver had met the family of FDR's first Secretary of Agriculture (and future Vice President) Henry A. Wallace in the 1890s while he was still a student at Iowa State University. Wallace credited Carver with inspiring his lifelong passion for plants and botany.

The devastation wrought by the storms that ravaged the Dust Bowl during the Great Depression made Carver's insightful work into soil conservation and crop rotation crucial. Although he and Wallace would later clash over agricultural practices, he remained a well-regarded expert in the field.

Carver also endeared himself to FDR because he researched the use of peanut oil-based massages as a treatment for polio. Roosevelt reportedly used Carver's massage technique, although later research debunked its efficacy.

When Carver died, Roosevelt signed legislation establishing the George Washington Carver National Monument in Missouri, the first non-presidential national monument and the first to honor a Black American.

He developed a close bond with Henry Ford.

It's perhaps unsurprising that science drew these two lifelong innovators to each other.

Henry Ford first sought out Carver's advice in the 1920s, beginning a friendship that lasted until Carver died in 1943. Ford was deeply interested in developing alternative energy sources to gasoline and was fascinated by Carver's work with soybeans and peanuts.

The two exchanged visits at Tuskegee and Ford's Dearborn, Michigan, plants, where they worked together on various initiatives.

During World War II, the U.S. government asked the pair to develop a soybean-based alternative to rubber during an era of wartime rationing. After weeks of experiments in Michigan in July 1942, Carver and Ford produced a successful replacement using goldenrod.

That same year, inspired by Carver's collaborations, Ford demonstrated a newly-designed car with a lightweight body comprised in part of soybeans. Ford also became a key financial backer of the Tuskegee Institute, underwriting many of Carver's initiatives and even installing an elevator in Carver's house to help his increasingly infirm friend move around his Alabama home.

Ford's fellow inventor Thomas Edison was also a fan of Carver.

Although Carver later embellished the story's financial details to reporters, in 1916, Edison unsuccessfully tried to lure Carver away from Tuskegee to become a researcher in Edison's famed New Jersey laboratory.

Carver even gave Gandhi nutritional advice.

Perhaps one of Carver's most unlikely friendships was with the man Carver affectionately called "My beloved friend, Mr. Gandhi." Their correspondence began in 1929 when Mahatma Gandhi was in his early years as the Indian independence movement leader.

A long-time vegetarian, Gandhi knew that his fight would be a long and arduous one, which could quickly sap his emotional and physical strength. So he reached out to Carver for nutritional advice, and the two struck up a friendship that lasted until at least 1935, with Carver preaching the benefits of adding soy to Gandhi's diet.

Carver even traveled to India to advise Gandhi on implementing his nutritional theories into India and other developing nations.

Gandhi wasn't the only foreign leader to seek Carver's help. Soviet leader Joseph Stalin, whose brutal agrarian reforms resulted in a famine that killed millions, asked Carver to visit the Soviet Union in the 1930s to reorganize a series of cotton plantations. Carver, however, refused Stalin's invitation, most likely because of his patriotism and his unwillingness to leave his beloved Tuskegee University.

George Washington Carver, full-length portrait, seated on steps, facing front, with staff. , ca. 1902.

George Washington Carver

Photo of George Washington Carver shaking hands with President Roosevelt

Dr. George Washington Carver with Henry Ford after being presented with a modern, fully equipped laboratory for food research, a gift from Mr. Ford.

22

Dr. Daniel Hale Williams: American medical pioneer

A look at Dr. Daniel Hale Williams' accomplishments will show a man who believed, *'If it aint been done, then do it.'*. He was committed to providing proper medical treatment and medical training to Black Americans at the turn of the Century despite many challenges. Dr. Williams did not let finances stop him. He made shoes, cut hair, and played the bass violin to earned money for his education.

When racial discrimination shut him out of professional medical societies, Dr. Williams helped form one. Even during medical school, he built Provident Hospital and opened the School of Nursing in Chicago. Provident was the first to be owned and operated by Blacks and the first to be non-segregated. Dr. Williams was a patriot who did this extraordinary feat to ensure that there would be opportunities for the increasing number of Black Americans in the medical field and dignity for Black patients. Rev. Fredrick Douglass, his cousin, helped him advocate and raise funds.

A little-known fact about the first open-heart surgery was that Dr. Williams performed it as an emergency. The patient had been stabbed in the chest, and the knife was still inserted. Dr. Williams and his team of fellow Black doctors had no heart-lung bypass machine to keep the blood and oxygen flowing; they had no blood transfusion capability and no antibiotics such as penicillin, which had not been discovered. No one had ever operated on a beating heart before this anywhere. The patient was named James Cornish, and he was released three months later.

The Martin Luther King Republicans encourage you to study more about Dr. Williams, who created a path for himself and others. The following profile was gathered from "Daniel Hale William's Marking Time" article in the *Pennsylvania Heritage Online Magazine*. The report highlights the historical marker installed by the *Pennsylvania Historical and Museum Commission (PHMC)* in Hollidaysburg, Pennsylvania in 1989.

Who was Dr. Daniel Hale Williams?

Daniel Hale Williams was born January 18, 1856, the son of Daniel and Sarah Ann Price Williams, in Hollidaysburg, Blair County. When his father died in 1867, his mother, who moved to Annapolis, Maryland, arranged an apprenticeship as a shoemaker for her son. Dissatisfied with shoe making, Williams later settled in Janesville, Wisconsin, along with his sister Sally. He found work at Harry Anderson's Tonsorial Parlor and Bathing Rooms, where the proprietor took the siblings into his home and encouraged Williams to complete his high school education.

Williams intended to pursue a career in law but declared it "quarrelsome." His interest in the medical profession grew while apprenticing for prominent Janesville physician Henry Palmer (1827–1895), chief surgeon of the U.S. Army Hospital at York during the American Civil War. In 1880, Williams enrolled in the prestigious Chicago Medical School, affiliated with Northwestern University and known today as the Feinberg School of Medicine. After graduating in 1883, his patients affectionately called him "Doctor Dan." Williams adapted the findings of germ theory promoted by French scientist Louis Pasteur (1822– 1895) and incorporated sterilization procedures learned in medical school. Dismayed by high mortality rates from infections in hospitals, he preferred operating during house calls.

After several nursing schools denied admission to a friend's sister because of her race, Williams sought the help of wealthy individuals, Black and White Americans. The following year, in 1891, he founded the Provident Hospital and Training School Association in Chicago as an interracial hospital and training school for Black American nurses.

In 1893, Williams operated and repaired the sac surrounding a young man's heart stabbed in a fight. On the claim that this was the first cardiac surgery ever performed, historians cited a similar stab wound case in St. Louis in 1891. Still, they agree that Williams was the first Black American to perform this procedure.

Williams became chief surgeon of Freedman's Hospital in Washington, D.C., in 1894. Established by the federal government to treat elderly and indigent Black Americans, he improved the hospital's quality of care, reduced its mortality rate, and found its medical school. Because the American Medical Association did not accept Black American members, Williams helped establish the National Medical Association in 1895. He received a role as the organization's vice president, declining the offer to be president.

Williams married Alice Johnson in 1898 and returned to Chicago, resuming duties at Provident Hospital. In 1912, he resigned after being accused of "disloyalty" to Provident by becoming an associate attending surgeon at Chicago's Saint Luke's Hospital. Today, affiliation with more than one hospital is common.

Williams performed 357 surgeries on ovarian cysts, reporting in 1901 that cysts were found in both Black and White patients. This discovery proved the prevailing medical belief that cysts did not occur in Black American women to be erroneous. He also successfully sutured a heavily bleeding spleen in 1902, one of the earliest of these procedures in medical history. His pioneering work in surgery, promoting medical education for Black American doctors and nurses, and improving care for people of all colors earned the Pennsylvania native a state historical marker installed by the Pennsylvania Historical and Museum Commission (PHMC) in 1989 at the location of his boyhood home on Blair Street in Hollidaysburg, today the site of the Blair County Court House. Daniel Hale Williams died in Idlewood, Michigan, on August 4, 1931.

Later photo of Daniel Hale Williams

An undated photograph of nurses in front of Provident Hospital at its second location at 36th and Dearborn Street, Chicago- Courtesy of Chicago History Museum

23

Supreme Justice Thurgood Marshall: Constitutional scholar and civil rights advocate

Thurgood Marshall was a patriot who used the Constitution serve his country in the courts and to destroy restrictive laws to help advance Black Americans. He has earned an important place in American history because of two significant accomplishments. First, as legal counsel for the National Association for the Advancement of Colored People (NAACP), he guided the litigation that broke the legal underpinnings of Jim Crow segregation. Second, as an associate justice of the Supreme Court–the nation's first Black justice in the highest court in the country.

When Marshall was a youth, he had to memorize the entire Constitution as a punishment for being an unruly student. This exercise imprinted the supreme law of this land in Marshall. Historian Paul Gewirtz considered him *"the country's greatest civil rights leader during the greatest period for civil rights advances in our history."* His victories were considered a vindication. Political scientist Christopher Vasillopulos wrote in <u>Prevailing Upon the American Dream: Thurgood Marshall and Brown v Board of Education,</u>

> *"Thurgood Marshall's victory was much more than the vindication of a life in service to the concept of equal justice under the law. It was vindication of Lincoln's Understanding of the the Constitution. It was a vindication of America."*

The Martin Luther King Republicans encourage you to learn the Constitution and read more about Justice Marshall's life. Also, visit the *Thurgood Marshall Memorial* in Annapolis on the old Court of Appeals building where Marshall argued some of his early civil rights cases. The Reader's Companion to American History is an excellent resource and where the following information is gathered.

Who was Justice Thurgood Marshall?

Thurgood Marshall was born on July 2, 1908, in Baltimore, Maryland. His father, William Marshall, the grandson of a slave, worked as a steward at an exclusive club. His mother, Norma, was a kindergarten teacher. One of William Marshall's favorite pastimes was to listen to cases at the local courthouse before returning home to rehash the arguments with his sons. Thurgood Marshall later recalled, *"Now you want to know how I got involved in law? I don't know. The nearest I can get is that my dad, my brother, and I had the most violent arguments you ever heard about anything. I guess we argued five out of seven nights at the dinner table."*

Marshall attended Baltimore's Colored High and Training School (later renamed Frederick Douglass High School), where he was an above-average student and put his finely honed skills of argument to use as a star member of the debate team. But, unfortunately, the teenage Marshall was also something of a mischievous troublemaker. His most remarkable high school accomplishment, memorizing the entire United States Constitution, was actually a teacher's punishment for misbehaving in class.

After graduating from high school in 1926, Marshall attended Lincoln University, a Historically Black College in Pennsylvania. There, he joined a remarkably distinguished student body that included Kwame Nkrumah, the future president of Ghana; Langston Hughes, the great poet; and Cab Calloway, the famous jazz singer.

After graduating from Lincoln with honors in 1930, Marshall applied to the University of Maryland Law School. Despite being overqualified academically, Marshall was rejected because of his race. This firsthand experience with discrimination in education made a lasting impression on Marshall and helped determine the future course of his career. Instead of Maryland, Marshall attended law school in Washington, D.C., at Howard University, another historically Black school. The dean of Howard Law School at the time was the pioneering civil rights lawyer Charles Houston. Marshall quickly fell under the tutelage of Houston, a notorious disciplinarian and extraordinarily demanding Thurgood Marshall argued thirty-two cases before the U.S. Supreme Court, more than anyone else in history.

Between 1934 and 1961, as an attorney for the NAACP, Marshall traveled throughout the United States, representing all manner of clients whenever a dispute involved questions of racial justice–from trials for common crimes to appellate advocacy raising the most intricate matters of constitutional law. His exploits earned him the appellation "Mr. Civil Rights." He argued thirty-two cases before the Supreme Court, prevailing in twenty-nine of them. These cases include Smith v. Allwright (1944), which invalidated the so-called White primary (the practice of barring Blacks from the Democratic party primary in a state where that party controlled state government), Shelley v. Kraemer (1948), which prohibited state courts from enforcing racially restrictive real estate covenants, and Brown v. Board of Education of Topeka, which invalidated state-enforced racial segregation in the public schools.

The next stage in Marshall's career consisted of a series of high-level appointments. In 1961, President John F. Kennedy appointed him to the U.S. Court of Appeals. In 1965, President Lyndon B. Johnson appointed him solicitor general, another racial "first." And in 1967, President Johnson appointed Marshall to the Supreme Court, declaring that it was *"the right thing to do, the right time to do it, the right man and the right place."*

No justice has been more libertarian in terms of opposing government regulation of speech or private sexual conduct. Nor has any justice been more egalitarian in advancing a view of the Constitution that imposes positive duties on the government to provide certain essential benefits to people—education, legal services, access to courts—regardless of their ability to pay for them.

George E.C. Hayes, left, Thurgood Marshall, center, and James M. Nabrit outside the U.S. Supreme Court in Washington, D.C., on May 17, 1954

TILLMAN'S HANDBOOK OF GREAT BLACK AMERICAN PATRIOTS

Justice Thurgood Marshall 1967

24

Dr. Ben Carson: American medical genius, HUD Secretary and presidential confidant

Dr. Ben Carson

The soft-spoken genius Dr. Ben Carson has stood as an example that hard work and dedication can lift a person out of whatever circumstance they're in. Dr. Carson's history of separating the Binder twins, running for President of the United States, and then becoming the 17th Secretary of the Department of Housing and Urban Development and advisor to the president are examples of what others think impossible, he gives a little more thought.

He is chosen to be among other great Black American patriots because his contributions to the nation have spanned two fields, medical and political. In each capacity, he believed in God, himself, and worked with others to change lives. In 2021, he and his wife Candy founded the *American Cornerstone Institute*. This organization uses principles of faith, liberty, community, and life to advocate for public policy. The Martin Luther King Republicans invite you to 'Think Big' and visit the exhibit at the *National Museum of African American History and Culture* in Washington, D.C., to learn more about Dr. Ben Carson. The profile included can found on *biography.com*.

Who is Dr. Ben Carson?

Ben Carson went from being a poor student to receiving academic honors and eventually attending medical school. As a doctor, he became director of pediatric neurosurgery at Johns Hopkins Hospital at age 33 and earned fame for his groundbreaking work separating conjoined twins. He retired from medicine in 2013, and two years later, he entered politics, making a bid to become the Republican candidate for U.S. president. Carson dropped out of the race in March 2016 and became a vocal supporter of Republican nominee Donald Trump, eventually earning selection as President Trump's Secretary of the Department of Housing and Urban Development.

Birth and Family Background

Carson was born in Detroit, Michigan, on September 18, 1951, the second son of Sonya and Robert Solomon Carson. His mother was raised in Tennessee in a huge family and dropped out of school in the third grade. She married Baptist minister and factory worker Robert Carson when she was 13. The couple moved to Detroit and had two children.

Influential Mother

After the couple divorced, Carson was eight, and Curtis, his brother, was 10; Sonya began to raise them as a single mother. Reportedly moving to Boston to live with her sister for a time and eventually returning to Detroit. The family was impoverished and, to make ends meet, Sonya sometimes toiled at two or three jobs simultaneously to provide for her boys.

As Carson later detailed in his autobiography, his mother was frugal with the family's finances, cleaning and patching clothes from the Goodwill to dress the boys. The family would also go to local farmers and offer to pick vegetables in exchange for a yield portion. Sonya would then can the produce for her boys' meals. Her actions and how she managed the family proved to be a tremendous influence on Carson and Curtis.

Sonya also taught her boys that anything was possible. By his recollection many years later, Carson had thoughts of a career in medicine. But, for medical care, his family would have to wait for hours to be seen by one of the interns at hospitals in Boston or Detroit. Carson observed the hospital as doctors and nurses went about their routines, dreaming that one day they would be calling for a "Dr. Carson."

Power of Reading

Both Carson and his brother experienced difficulty in school. Carson fell to the bottom of his class and became the object of ridicule by his classmates. Determined to turn her sons around, Sonya limited their TV time to a few select programs and refused to let them go outside to play until they had finished their homework.

She required them to read two library books a week and give her written reports, even though she could barely read them with her poor education. At first, Carson resented the strict regimen. Still, after several weeks, he began to find enjoyment in reading, discovering he could go anyplace, be anybody and do anything between the covers of a book.

Carson began to learn how to use his imagination and found it more enjoyable than watching television. This attraction to reading soon led to a strong desire to learn more. Carson read literature about all types of subjects, seeing himself as the central character of what he was reading, even if it was a technical book or an encyclopedia.

Carson would later say that he began to view his prospects differently. He could become the scientist or physician he had dreamed about, and thus, he cultivated an academic focus. A fifth-grade science teacher was one of the first to encourage Carson's interests in lab work after he was the only student able to identify an obsidian rock sample brought to school.

Within a year, Carson amazed his teachers and classmates with his academic improvement. He recalled facts and examples from his books at home and related them to what he was learning in school.

Still, there were challenges. After Carson received a certificate of achievement in the eighth grade for being at the top of his class, a teacher openly berated his fellow white students for letting a Black boy get ahead of them academically.

At Southwestern High School in inner-city Detroit, Carson's science teachers recognized his intellectual abilities and mentored him further. Other educators helped him to stay focused when outside influences pulled him off course.

Burgeoning Surgical Career

Carson graduated with honors from Southwestern, becoming a senior commander in the school's ROTC program. He earned a full scholarship to Yale, receiving a B.A. degree in psychology in 1973.

Carson enrolled in the School of Medicine at the University of Michigan, choosing to become a neurosurgeon. In 1975, he married Lacena "Candy" Rustin, whom he met at Yale. Carson earned his medical degree, and the young couple moved to Baltimore, Maryland, where he became an intern at Johns Hopkins University in 1977. His excellent eye-hand coordination and three-dimensional reasoning skills made him a superior surgeon early on. By 1982, he was chief resident in neurosurgery at Hopkins.

In 1983, Carson received an important invitation. Sir Charles Gairdner Hospital in Perth, Australia, needed a neurosurgeon and invited Carson to take the position. Resistant at first to move so far away from home, he eventually accepted the offer. It proved to be an important one. Australia at the time was lacking doctors with highly sophisticated training in neurosurgery. Carson gained several years' worth of experience in the year he was at Gairdner Hospital and honed his skills tremendously.

Carson returned to Johns Hopkins in 1984 and, by 1985, he became director of pediatric neurosurgery at the age of 33, at the time, the youngest U.S. physician to hold such a position. In 1987, Carson attracted international attention by performing a surgery to separate 7-month-old occipital craniopagus twins in Germany.

Patrick and Benjamin Binder were born joined at the head. Their parents contacted Carson, who went to Germany to consult with the family and the boys' doctors. Because the boys were joined at the back of the head, he felt he could be successful because they had separate brains.

On September 4, 1987, after months of rehearsals, Carson and a vast team of doctors, nurses, and support staff joined forces for what would be a 22-hour procedure. Part of the challenge in radical neurosurgery is to prevent severe bleeding and trauma to the patients. In the highly complex operation, Carson had applied both hypothermic and circulatory arrest. Although the twins did suffer some brain damage and post-operation bleeding, both survived the separation, allowing Carson's surgery to be considered by the medical establishment the first successful procedure of its kind.

Separating Conjoined Twins

In 1994, Carson and his team went to South Africa to separate the Makwaeba twins. The operation was unsuccessful, as both girls died from complications of the surgery. Carson was devastated but vowed to press on, as he knew such procedures could be successful. In 1997, Carson and his team went to Zambia in South Central Africa to separate infant boys, Luka and Joseph Banda. This operation was complicated because the boys were joined at the tops of their heads, facing in opposite directions, making it the first time a surgery of this type had been performed. After a 28-hour operation supported by previously rendered 3-D mapping, both boys survived, and neither suffered brain damage.

Over time, Carson's operations began to gain media attention. At first, what people saw was the soft-spoken surgeon explaining complicated procedures in simple terms. But in time, Carson's own story became public—a troubled youth growing up in the inner city to a low-income family eventually finding success.

Soon, Carson began traveling to schools, businesses, and hospitals across the country, telling his story and imparting his philosophy of life. Out of this dedication to education and helping young people, Carson and his wife founded the Carson Scholars Fund in 1994. The foundation grants scholarships to students and promotes reading in the younger grades.

Biggest Medical Challenge

In 2003, Carson faced what was perhaps his biggest challenge: separating adult conjoined twins. Ladan and Laleh Bijani were Iranian women who were joined at the head. For 29 years, they had literally lived together in every conceivable way. Like normal twins, they shared experiences and outlooks, including earning law degrees, but as they got older and developed their own individual aspirations, they knew they could never lead independent lives unless they separated. As they told Carson at one point, "We would rather die than spend another day together."

This type of medical procedure had never been attempted on conjoined adults because of the dangerous outcomes. By this time, Carson had been conducting brain surgery for nearly 20 years and had performed several craniopagus separations. He later stated he tried to talk the two women out of the surgery, but after many discussions with them and consultations with many other doctors and surgeons, he agreed to proceed.

Carson and a team of more than 100 surgeons, specialists, and assistants traveled to Singapore in Southeast Asia. On July 6, 2003, Carson and his team began the nearly 52-hour operation. They again relied on a 3-D imaging technique that Carson had utilized to prepare for the Banda twins' operation. The computerized images allowed the medical team to conduct a virtual surgery before the operation. During the procedure, they followed digital reconstructions of the twins' brains.

The surgery revealed more difficulties outside of the girls' ages; their brains not only shared a major vein but had fused together. The separation was completed during the afternoon of July 8. But it was soon apparent that the girls were in deep critical condition.

At 2:30 p.m., Ladan died on the operating table. Her sister Laleh died a short time later. The loss was devastating to all, especially Carson, who stated that the girls' bravery to pursue the operation had contributed to neurosurgery in ways that would live far beyond them.

Because of his unflagging dedication to children and his many medical breakthroughs, Carson has received a legion of honorary doctorate degrees and accolades and has sat on the boards of numerous business and education boards.

Cancer Diagnosis, Books and Movie

In 2002, Carson was forced to cut back on his breakneck pace after developing prostate cancer. He took an active role in his own case, reviewing X-rays and consulting with the team of surgeons who operated on him. Carson fully recovered from the operation cancer-free. The brush with death caused him to adjust his life to spend more time with his wife and their three children, Murray, Benjamin Jr. and Rhoeyce.

After his recovery, Carson still kept a busy schedule, conducting operations and speaking to various groups around the country. He has also written several books, including the popular autobiography *Gifted Hands* (1990). Other titles include—*Think Big* (1992), *The Big Picture* (1999), and *Take the Risk* (2007)—are about his personal philosophies on learning, success, hard work, and religious faith.

In 2000, the Library of Congress selected Carson as one of its "Living Legends." The following year, CNN and *Time* magazine named Carson as one of the nation's 20 foremost physicians and scientists. In 2006, he received the Spingarn Medal, the highest honor bestowed by the NAACP. In February 2008, President George W. Bush awarded Carson the Ford's Theatre Lincoln Medal and the Presidential Medal of Freedom. And in 2009, actor Cuba Gooding Jr. portrayed Carson in the television production *Gifted Hands*.

Presidential Run

As Carson focused more on politics than on medicine, he became known as an outspoken conservative Republican. In 2012, he published *America the Beautiful: Rediscovering What Made This Nation Great*. In February 2013, Carson attracted attention for his speech at the National Prayer Breakfast. He criticized President Barack Obama for his positions on taxation and healthcare.

The following month he announced that he was officially retiring from his career as a surgeon. That October, he was hired by Fox News in October 2013 to work as a contributor. Then in May 2014, Carson published his No. 1 *New York Times* bestseller *One Nation: What We Can All Do To Save America's Future*.

On May 4, 2015, Carson launched his official bid for the Republican presidential nomination at an event in Detroit. *"I'm not a politician,"* Carson said. *"I don't want to be a politician because politicians do what is politically expedient. I want to do what's right."*

During the Campaign and the End of the Trail

With a crowded field of contenders, Carson was one of the 10 top candidates who participated in a Fox News presidential debate in early August.

Over the ensuing months, Carson rose through the ranks to become a leading contender among the nominees against outspoken rival Donald Trump and was seen as a favorite among evangelicals. (Carson is a Seventh Day Adventist.) In October, he also released another book, *A More Perfect Union*.

On March 2, 2016, Carson announced that he saw no path forward in his campaign and chose not to attend the Republican debate on March 3, in his hometown of Detroit. The next afternoon, at the CPAC (Conservative Political Action Conference), he spoke before an enthusiastic crowd about his values and the issues he felt important in the current campaign. He thanked his campaign staff and volunteers, especially Branden Joplin, an Iowa staffer who was killed in a car crash during the Iowa caucuses. He then stated, "I'm leaving the campaign trail." There was a softened moan from the crowd, then a standing ovation.

As the campaign continued, Carson became one of Trump's most loyal supporters, stumping for him around the country leading up to the election. On November 8, 2016, Trump was elected the 45th president of the United States, winning the majority of electoral college votes.

HUD Secretary

On December 5, 2016, Trump announced he was nominating Carson as the Secretary of the Department of Housing and Urban Development (HUD). *"Ben Carson has a brilliant mind and is passionate about strengthening communities and families within those communities,"* Trump said in a statement.

Despite Democratic opponents' concerns, the Senate Banking, Housing, and Urban Affairs Committee unanimously approved Carson's nomination on January 24, 2017. The Senate confirmed his nomination in a 58-41 vote on March 2, 2017.

His achievements at HUD helped spur greater economic opportunities for low-income families and revitalized many under-served communities. Some accomplishments during his tenure include saving $2.7 million, helping disaster victims recover, and reducing homelessness among extremely vulnerable populations.

In March 2019, Carson told Newsmax TV that he planned to leave his HUD post at the conclusion of President Trump's first term. *"I would be interested in returning to the private sector because I think you have just as much influence, maybe more, there,"* he said.

Young Ben Carson

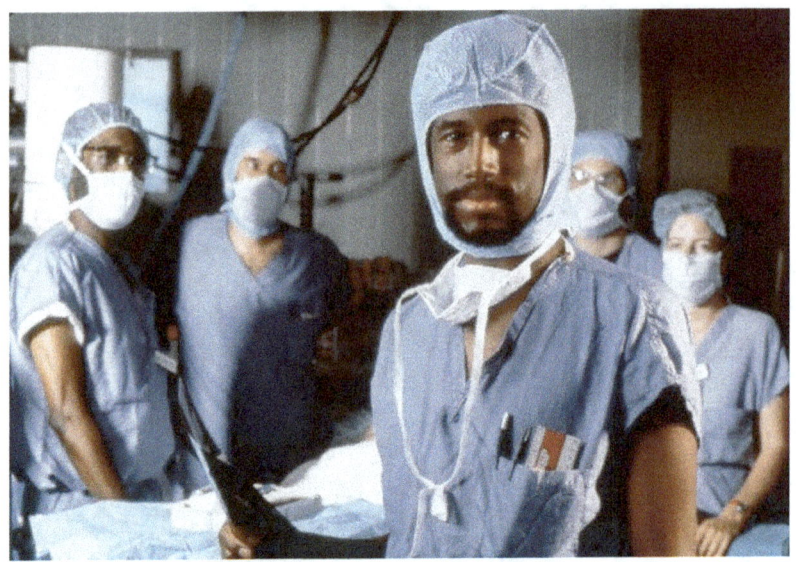

*Ben Carson with a Johns Hopkins surgical team in an undated photo.
Credit via Johns Hopkins Medicine*

Dr. Ben Carson official portrait as HUD secretary

25

Rev. Dr. Martin Luther King, Jr's Mountain Top sermon inspired by the Bible and Constitution

REV. DR. MARTIN LUTHER KING, JR'S MOUNTAIN TOP SERMON...

    The Martin Luther King Republicans are proud to carry on Dr. King's legacy using the Principals and Steps of Non Violence in our advocacy for peace and understanding among all Americans. We recognize this leader as a man ahead of his time, a Black American Patriot.

    Dr. King loved America and charged this country to stand on its foundation, the Constitution. In 1955, he demonstrated to the Interstate Commerce Commission its rule that segregation on interstate trains and buses and in waiting rooms used by interstate travelers violates the Interstate Commerce Act. Reversing this unconstitutional rule is the reason why the lunch counters opened up. The fake narrative that 'they marched, sang, got beat and got freedom' has led many to believe that Blacks did not have the right to vote until Dr. King led the march to Selma.

As citizens of America, Blacks most certainly had the 'right to vote.' But, unfortunately, southern political forces unjustly infringed on those rights. I am proud that in 1965, my mother, Dorothy Wright Tillman, along with others, fought against broad-spread voter suppression and terror being committed by the Southern Democrats. She was among those brave and peaceful protesters that were beaten on Edmund Pettis Bridge on Bloody Sunday.

No Black History Month will be complete without honoring our organization's namesake. Everyone has read an account of Rev. Dr. Martin Luther King Jr.'s life and accomplishments, so we will share his patriotic attributes. Dr. King understood as a citizen, he could petition the government and did not allow partisanship to be a factor. He used all aspects of the first amendment; freedom of speech, religion, press, assembly, and the right to petition the government. We encourage you to study more about Dr. King's use of the Constitution to create change. This chapter discusses Dr. King's last and most famous speech and his reference to the Constitution. Those interested can find the article on the *National Constitution Center* website, where we gather the following information. All Americans should also recognize the King family for keeping Dr. & Mrs. King's legacy available for us with the *King Center* in Atlanta, Georgia, and we encourage you to visit and make a donation.

How did Dr. King use the Constitution?

On April 3, 1968, Dr. Martin Luther King Jr. made his last public speech, which referenced the Bible and the Constitution. His words still inspire millions today.

King was in Memphis, Tennessee, to help support a sanitation workers' strike. At the age of 39, he was already an internationally known figure. Starting with the Montgomery boycott in 1955, King had led a series of nonviolent protests against discrimination.

King spoke at the Bishop Charles Mason Temple to a group of supporters–knowing publicly made threats against his life.

The best-known part of King's speech was its conclusion.

> *"Like anybody, I would like to live a long life–longevity has its place. But I'm not concerned about that now. I just want to do God's will. And He's allowed me to go up to the mountain. And I've looked over and I've seen the Promised Land. I may not get there with you. But I want you to know tonight, that we, as a people, will get to the Promised Land. And so I'm happy tonight; I'm not worried about anything; I'm not fearing any man. Mine eyes have seen the glory of the coming of the Lord,"*

King said as he ended the speech. The "we, as a people" reference, in conclusion, wasn't the only constitutional reference in his speech.

As you read the Mountaintop speech's text, King gives an inspirational history of the civil rights movement and places it in the context of the ages and the late 20th Century. He then turns his attention to an injunction against the protesting sanitation workers.

> *"We have an injunction and we're going into court tomorrow morning to fight this illegal, unconstitutional injunction. All we*

say to America is, "Be true to what you said on paper." If I lived in China or even Russia, or any totalitarian country, maybe I could understand some of these illegal injunctions," King said.

"Maybe I could understand the denial of certain basic First Amendment privileges, because they hadn't committed themselves to that over there. But somewhere I read of the freedom of assembly. Somewhere I read of the freedom of speech. Somewhere I read of the freedom of press. Somewhere I read that the greatness of America is the right to protest for right. And so just as I say, we aren't going to let dogs or water hoses turn us around, we aren't going to let any injunction turn us around. We are going on."

The First Amendment right to peacefully protest was an integral part of King's success in the civil rights movement. Later in the speech, King describes how the protesters can use an economic boycott to message peacefully.

He also told the audience how he survived a 1958 assassination attempt by a mentally deranged woman who stabbed King in the chest at a New York book signing. King had read in a newspaper that if he had sneezed just before the attack, the wound's location has been fatal.

"I want to say tonight that I, too, am happy that I didn't sneeze. Because if I had sneezed I wouldn't have been around here in 1960, when students all over the South started sitting-in at lunch counters. And I knew that as they were sitting in, they were really standing up for the best in the American dream and taking the whole nation back to those great wells of democracy, which were dug deep by the founding fathers in the Declaration of Independence and the Constitution," he said.

At 6:05 P.M. on Thursday, April 4, 1968, King was shot while standing on a balcony outside his second-floor room at the Lorraine Motel. One shot was heard coming from another location. King was rushed to a hospital and died an hour later.

Martin Luther King, Jr. leaves the West Wing after meeting with President Johnson. August 5, 1965

Pres. Johnson meets with Civil Rights leaders Martin Luther King, Jr., Whitney Young, and James Farmer in the Oval Office. January 18, 1964

Dr. King at Mason Temple (Photo by Vernon Matthews / The Commercial Appeal)

26

Dr. Carter G. Woodson: Father of Black History Month

DR. CARTER G. WOODSON: FATHER OF BLACK HISTORY MONTH

We conclude this Black History Month with the man who started it all, Dr. Carter G. Woodson. What began as Negro History Week has become a national education celebration. In the summer of 1915, Dr. Woodson attended a commemoration of the 50th Anniversary of Emancipation sponsored by Illinois. Inspired by the three-week festival, Woodson decided to form an organization to promote the scientific study of Black life and history before leaving Chicago. By the fall, Woodson with A. L. Jackson and three others formed the Association for the Study of Negro Life and History.

In 1926, at the Wabash YMCA located 3757 S.Wabash in Chicago, Dr.

Woodson initiated the celebration of Negro History Week in February, which corresponded with the birthdays of Frederick Douglass and Abraham Lincoln.

Black History Month was put forward to Black students and educators across the nation in 1969, and the first celebration took place at Kent University in 1970. However, it wasn't until 1976 when President Gerald Ford officially recognized Black History Month. In honor of all the work that this patriot has done to promote the study of Black American History, an ornament of Dr. Woodson hangs on the White House's Christmas tree each year. We encourage you to explore the scholarly writings of Dr. Woodson and to visit the *Carter G. Woodson National Historic Site* in Washington, DC, where we gathered this information.

> *"Do not let the role which you have played be obscured while others write themselves into the foreground of your story." -Dr. Carter G. Woodson*

Who was Dr. Carter G. Woodson?

Born on December 19, 1875, in New Canton, Virginia, Carter Godwin Woodson was the fourth of nine children born to parents who had been enslaved. As a Black American boy growing up in central Virginia during the late 19th century in the Reconstruction Era, Woodson had few educational or employment opportunities. In pursuit of a new life, he and his family moved to Huntington, West Virginia, where he worked in the New River Gorge coalfields to supplement the family's income. Finally, at the age of 20, Woodson saved enough money from his days as a coal miner to begin his formal education at Frederick Douglass High School in Huntington, one of the few Black high schools at the time. He received his diploma in just two years, as he was already self-taught in basic reading, writing, and arithmetic. Woodson earned his first collegiate degree from Berea College in Berea, Kentucky, in 1903 and continued his education at the University of Chicago, obtaining another Bachelor's degree and a Master's degree, both in 1908. In 1912, he earned his Ph.D. in History from Harvard University, making him the second Black American (only following W.E.B. DuBois) to graduate with a Ph.D. from Harvard; and the only person of enslaved parentage to earn a Ph.D. in History from any institution in the United States.

Around the turn of the 20th century, as he began his academic career, Woodson noticed a glaring hole in the United States' educational system. The public knew very little about Black Americans' role in American history, and schools were not including Black American history in their curriculum. He worked tirelessly throughout his life to remedy this problem, becoming recognized as "the Father of Black History."

Institutionalizing the Field of Black History

As Woodson immersed himself in the world of education, he noticed the prevailing ignorance and lack of information concerning Black life and history. In an attempt to correct such an apparent oversight, Woodson, on September 9, 1915, co-founded the Association for the Study of Negro Life and History, Inc., now known as the Association for the Study of African American Life and History, Inc. (ASALH). The organization aimed to inform the American public about Black Americans' contributions to the country's formation, history, and culture. On July 18, 1922, Woodson purchased his home at 1538 Ninth Street, N.W. in Washington, D.C., and he located the association's headquarters on the first floor. He resided on the third floor of the home until his death on April 3, 1950.

While running the organization, Woodson also took on many

other roles within the academic world. He taught at both the public school and collegiate levels, trained researchers and other staff at the organization, and wrote books and articles on the subject that was his life's work. In addition, Woodson held the position of Dean at the School of Liberal Arts and Head of the Graduate Faculty at Howard University from 1919 to 1920. He also served as Dean at West Virginia Collegiate Institute, now known as West Virginia State University. Although he was well-respected and sought after in the academic arena, Woodson retired from teaching in 1922 to devote his full attention to ASALH, research, writing, and grooming young scholars for the historical profession.

Woodson also started the academic publication *The Journal of Negro History* in 1916 and *The Negro History Bulletin* in 1937. In 1921, he founded the Associated Publishers, Inc. This publishing company took on works that other companies would not, such as Black scholars and women's writings on Black American and African Diaspora history.

A Champion of Women and a Mentor to Many

During Woodson's lifetime, the association had five presidents. In 1936, Mary McLeod Bethune was elected president of the organization, filling the vacancy left open after educator John Hope's death. Bethune was not only the first female president; she was also its longest-serving, wearing the title until 1952. Unlike most male scholars during this time, Woodson welcomed Black American women as equal co-workers and leaders in the ranks of his movement and facilitated productive cross-generational dialogues and relationships. He was a mentor to many up-and-coming historians and scholars such as Alrutheus A. Taylor, Luther Porter Jackson, Lorenzo Johnston Greene, Rayford W. Logan, Lawrence D. Reddick, John Hope Franklin and Central State University's founding president Charles H. Wesley. The association's headquarters/Woodson's office-home served as a training center, and these scholars, in turn, trained succeeding generations of Black American historians that helped legitimize Black history. While Woodson developed young men and women, the association developed essential relationships with Black churches, colleges, universities, schools, and community centers all around the country.

Woodson at work in his study, circa 1940s.

Dr. Mary McLeod Bethune, Lucy Harth Smith, and Dr. Carter G. Woodson at ASALH's Annual Conference in Chicago, Illinois 1940.

II

National Parks and Landmarks, Statues, Museums, & Historic Places

The following list is in alphabetical order beginning with the first letter of location name.

27

Places to visit

Across the United States, there are numerous National Parks and Landmarks, statues, museums, and historical places dedicated to notable Black Americans. These places demonstrate how America has honored and celebrated these figures and recognize their historical significance. Moreover, they provide future generations a reminder that Black Americans have always been a part of the growth and transformation of this young country; through challenges, they have remained committed to seeing America live up to its founding principles.

This chapter includes an abbreviated list of places dedicated to those mentioned in *Tillman's Handbook of Great Black American Patriots.* The reader is encouraged to visit these places and study more about these patriots.

African American Civil War Memorial

1925 Vermont Ave NW
  Washington, DC 20024
  (202) 426-6841

More than 200,000 African-American soldiers and sailors served in the US Army and Navy during the American Civil War. Their contribution helped to end the war and free over four million slaves. The African American Civil War Memorial honors their service and sacrifice.

African American Civil War Memorial

African American Civil War Memorial Museum

1925 Vermont Avenue, NW
Washington, DC
This national memorial commemorates the 209,145 soldiers of the US Colored Troops. Their names are inscribed on the Wall of Honor alongside the Spirit of Freedom sculpture by Ed Hamilton. The adjacent museum and research center conveys the USCT story

and Black American military history through exhibits, re-enactments, and dynamic programs.

American Revolution Museum at Yorktown

200 Water Street, Route 1020
Yorktown, VA 23690
The American Revolution Museum at Yorktown tells the story of the nation's founding, from the colonial period to the dawn of the Constitution and beyond. It houses the *African Americans and the American Revolution* exhibit.

Ben Carson Exhibit

Smithsonian National Museum of African American History & Culture
1400 Constitution Ave NW
Washington, DC
Visitors can see Dr. Ben Carson's accomplishments inside the Smithsonian National Museum of African American History & Culture *Making a Way Out of No Way* exhibit.

Benjamin Banneker National Park

Between I-395, Maine Avenue, and 9th Street SW
Washington, DC.
The National Park Service is the steward of the eight-acre park that commemorates the Black American scientist, surveyor, and author who helped the survey of the District of Columbia's original boundaries. Landscape architect Dan Kiley designed the park, which opened in 1967.

Benjamin Banneker Historical Park and Museum

300 Oella Avenue
Baltimore, Maryland
(410) 887-1081

Benjamin Banneker Historical Park and Museum is a beautiful 142-acre site showcasing Banneker's contributions and is the location is where Banneker wrote his almanacs and famous letter to Thomas Jefferson. Banneker also crafted one of the first all-American-made wooden clocks here.

Benjamin Banneker and the Boundary Stones of the District of Columbia

National Historic Landmark
Arlington, Virginia

Today an iron fence surrounds the SW-9 Intermediate Boundary Stone, which is approximately 15 inches tall. It is a sandstone slab one-foot square. With few places left associated with Banneker, this boundary stone goes far beyond marking the former borders of Washington, DC. It and the other remaining boundary stones also serve as monuments to the life pursuits of a self-educated man who advanced scientific inquiry in colonial America.

Benjamin Banneker and the Boundary Stones of the District of Columbia

Bishop Richard Allen Museum

419 S 6th St
 Philadelphia, PA 19147
 (215) 925-0616

The Richard Allen Museum is housed in the Mother Bethel AME Church basement, which stands on the oldest parcel of land continuously owned by African-Americans and is the first AME church site. Ring the bell at the side door, and a docent will lead you on a tour of the museum, where you can learn Richard Allen's story, visit his remains in the crypt, and see artifacts from the early church (including Allen's Bible and his wife's ledger book, used to record rent income). The tour finishes up in the sanctuary, with its gorgeous stained glass windows and wood-beamed ceiling.

Bishop Richard Allen statue outside Mother Bethel in Philadelphia

Booker T. Washington National Monument

12130 Booker T. Washington Highway
Hardy, VA 24101
(540) 721-2094

Booker T. Washington was born in slavery on this 207-acre tobacco farm. From 1946 to 1951, Congress authorized the Booker T. Washington Memorial a half dollar to support the site's purchase. The area was designated a National Monument in 1956 and listed on the National Register of Historic Places in 1966. The monument illustrates Washington's life and achievements and the 1850s slavery and farming through gardens, buildings, crafts, and animals.

Boston African American National Historic Site

15 State Street
Boston, MA 02109
(617) 742-5415

The Boston African American National Historic Site is the most significant pre-Civil War Black-owned structure in the United States. It is comprised of 24 sites on the north side of Beacon Hill. This group of historic buildings was the homes, schools, churches, and businesses of a thriving Black community. The sites are connected by the 1.6 miles (2.5 km) Black Heritage Trail.

Boston Massacre/Crispus Attucks Monument

Boston Common between Tremont Street and Avery Street
Boston, Massachusetts

The Boston Massacre / Crispus Attucks monument honors the victims of the Boston Massacre. Standing 25 feet high and 10 feet wide, a figure representing the Spirit of the Revolution holds a broken chain in her right hand, and in her left hand, she has the American flag. Her right foot crushes the crown of the British monarchy, and next to her other foot, an eagle prepares to fly. The names of the five martyrs: Crispus Attucks, James Caldwell, Patrick Carr, Samuel Gray, and Samuel Maverick are on the top of the column and behind the Spirit of the Revolution in raised letters. The monument's base portrays a relief of the Boston Massacre with the date March 5, 1770.

Boston Massacre/Crispus Attucks Monument

Boston Women Memorial

Commonwealth Avenue Mall
 Boston, MA 02116

The statue of Phillis Wheatley is one of three women subjects of the Boston Women's Memorial on Commonwealth Avenue Mall between Fairfield Street and Gloucester Street dedicated in 2003.

Statue of Phillis Wheatley in Boston

Bunker Hill National Monument

Monument Square
Charleston, Massachusetts 02129
This monument that was built in the mid-19th century stands atop Breed's Hill. It is the site where most of the fighting in the 1775 Battle of Bunker Hill happened and was designated a historic place in 1961.

Carter G. Woodson Home/Office National Historic Site

National Capital Parks-East
1900 Anacostia Drive SE
Washington, DC 20020
(202) 426-5961
This phone number is also listed for the Frederick Douglass National Historic Site, which staffs the Carter G. Woodson Home National Historic Site.

In 1976, the nation declared Dr. Carter G. Woodson's home office a National Historic Landmark. Following a 2003 Congressional Act, this home was named a National Historic Site, and in 2006 the Carter G. Woodson Home became the 389th unit of the National Park System.

Carter G. Woodson Residence

1538 Ninth Street, NW
Washington, DC
Carter G. Woodson devoted his life to the study and promotion of African American history. Here Woodson founded the Association for the Study of Negro Life and History in 1915, the Journal of Negro History in 1916, the Associated Publishers in 1921, and the Negro History Bulletin in 1937. Woodson, along with Omega Psi

Phi Fraternity, launched Negro History Week (now Black History Month) in 1926. He taught at M Street High School and served as a Howard University dean. A prolific writer with a Ph.D. in history from Harvard University (1912), Woodson influenced generations of scholars, activists, and artists.

Charles Richard Drew Memorial Marker

Haw River, North Carolina

The granite and bronze Charles Drew Memorial Marker was erected by Alamance County, Omega Psi Phi Fraternity, Inc., and private donors in 1986. It is located off NC 49 in an area across the road from where Dr. Drew had his fatal accident.

PLACES TO VISIT

Charles Richard Drew Memorial Marker

Charles Drew House

2505 1st Street
  Arlington, Virginia
  Dr. Charles Drew lived in this house from 1920 to 1939. After its nomination by the Afro-American Bicentennial Corporation, the National Park Service designated the house as a National Historic Landmark in 1976.

Cowpens National Battlefield

338 New Pleasant Road
Gaffney, SC 29341
(864) 461-2828

Cowpens National Battlefield is a National Park Service unit just east of Chesnee, South Carolina, and near the state line with North Carolina. It preserves a major battlefield of the American Revolutionary War and highlights the Black American Patriots who fought and died here.

Daniel Hale Williams Historical Marker

Blair, 300 Block & Wayne Street
Hollidaysburg, Pennsylvania

The site of Dr. Daniel Hale Williams's boyhood home was recognized by the Pennsylvania Historical and Museum Commission, which erected the marker in 1989.

Daniel Hale Williams Home- Chicago

445 E. 42nd Street
Chicago, IL

The Daniel Hale Williams House is listed in the National Register of Historic Places and was designated a National Historic Landmark in 1975. This location is not far from where I grew up in Chicago's Grand Boulevard neighborhood, where many notable Black Americans lived.

Daniel Hale Williams Home- Chicago

Daniel Hale Williams Home and Historical Marker - Idlewild

15712 Lake Drive
Idlewild, MI

Dr. Daniel Hale Williams (1858 1931) and his wife Alice (1866 1924) were among Idlewilds earliest residents. Williams's stature as a leading Chicago physician encouraged other Black professionals to spend leisure time here. The Williamses built this cottage, Oakmere, with its laboratory around 1920. When Dr. Dan died at Oakmere in 1931, all activities in Idlewild were canceled for the day. Williams left much of his estate to the NAACP, hospitals, and medical schools. The historical marker was erected in 2009

DC Recorder of Deeds Building/WPA Era Murals

515 D Street, NW
Washington, Dc

The Recorder of Deeds building, which houses the city's land records, is one of the city's Art Deco/Art Moderne landmarks, completed in 1941. Black Americans have served as recorders of deeds since President James A. Garfield appointed Frederick Douglass in 1881. Ten other Black Americans would succeed Douglass. Elocutionist Henrietta Vinton Davis became the first Black woman employed in the office in 1878, later serving as Douglass's assistant. In addition to portraits of the recorders of deeds and Selma Burke's bronze relief of President Franklin D. Roosevelt, the building is distinguished by a series of seven Works Projects Administration era murals on the theme of "the contribution of the Negro to the American Nation," including the 54th Massachusetts Regiment, astronomer Benjamin Banneker, and explorer Matthew A. Henson.

PLACES TO VISIT

DuBois Boyhood Home site Great Barrington

National Historic Landmark
612 S Egremont Rd
Great Barrington, MA 01230
(413) 717-6259

For a sixtieth birthday in 1928, friends at the NAACP gave DuBois the Burghardt family homestead. Although he wanted to renovate his grandfather's house, DuBois never had the funds and had to sell the property. The house was demolished in 1954. In 1967 the idea for a national memorial to Dr. DuBois was born when Professor Edmund W. Gordon and Walter Wilson, a local realtor, purchased the Home site property, establishing the DuBois Memorial Foundation a year later. The five-acre parcel includes the original Burghardt family homestead where DuBois spent his early boyhood. In 1987 the DuBois Memorial Foundation donated the National Historic Landmark to the Commonwealth of Massachusetts, designating the University of Massachusetts, Amherst, as custodian. The Homesite is an active teaching and research site for students and faculty at the UMass Amherst Anthropology Department.

Fredrick Douglass National Historic Site

1411 W Street SE
Washington, DC, 20020
(202) 426-5961

The Fredrick Douglass National Historic Site was established in 1988. Douglass lived in this house, named Cedar Hill, from 1877-1888 until 1895. The Frederick Douglass National Historic Site provides guided tours and exhibits.

Frederick Douglass Memorial

Central Park
New York City, New York
The Fredrick Douglass Memorial was dedicated on September 20, 2011. It is an 8-foot bronze sculpture depicting Douglass and a large circle and fountain located on New York Central Park's northwest corner. Harlem-based artist Algernon Miller designed a complex colored paving pattern that alludes to traditional African American quilt designs. Additional features, including wrought-iron symbolic and decorative elements, a water wall, and inscribed historical details and quotations, create a rich tableau representing the life of Douglass and the slaves' passage to freedom.

Rev. Fredrick Douglass Memorial

Frederick Douglass Museum and Cultural Center

3200 Wayman Avenue
Highland Beach, MD 21403
Twin Oaks, the summer cottage built for Rev. Fredrick Douglass in 1895 by his youngest son Major Charles Douglass, is home to the Frederick Douglass Museum and Cultural Center, Inc. It is located in Highland Beach, the 1st incorporated Black town in Maryland. Unfortunately, Rev. Douglass passed before moving into the cottage. It remained in the family until being purchased and restored in the 1980s. In 1995, the State of Maryland and Anne Arundel County acquired the home and deeded it to the Town of Highland Beach as a memorial to Frederick Douglass.

Frederick Douglass Museum and Hall of Fame for Caring Americans

320 A Street, NE
Washington, DC
(202) 547-4273
Frederick Douglass (ca. 1818–1895), the leading Black statesman of his time, lived the last 25 years of his life in Washington. In 1870 he arrived from Rochester, New York, as the corresponding editor of the New Era newspaper. Douglass and his wife Anna Murray Douglass lived in 316 A Street and later purchased 318. In 1877 they moved to Cedar Hill in Anacostia. Numbers 316, 318, and 320 became the Museum of African Art in 1964, the first US museum of its kind. In 1987 the museum—now the Smithsonian's National Museum of African Art—moved to the National Mall. Today the houses serve as the Frederick Douglass Museum and Hall of Fame for Caring Americans.

PLACES TO VISIT

Frederick Douglass Memorial Plaza

Highland Park
Rochester, New York
The Rochester community installed this statute of Rev. Fredrick Douglass in Rochestester, New York, in 1899. It was the 1st statute in the United States that memorized a specific Black American. In 2019 it was relocated to the Fredrick Douglass Memorial Plaza.

Freedmen's Hospital, African American Heritage Trail

2041 Georgia Ave NW,
Washington, DC 20060
(202)355-4280
Freedmen's Hospital, the predecessor to Howard University Hospital, was established during the Civil War to address the needs of thousands of Black Americans who poured into the city seeking freedom. Organizers quickly incorporated an initiative of the federal government into Howard University, eventually developing into a first-rate medical campus. The current building on the site is the Seeley G. Mudd Building of the Howard University College of Medicine, containing classrooms and offices.

Freedom's Way National Heritage Area-Barzillai exhibit

94 Jackson Road, Suite 311
Devens, MA 01434
(978) 772.3654
Designated by Congress in 2009, Freedom's Way National Heritage Area encompasses 45 communities in north-central Massachusetts and southern New Hampshire that are steeped in history, natural

beauty, and the legacy of revolutionary ideas. As a National Heritage Area, Freedom's Way NHA is managed by Freedom's Way Heritage Association.

George Washington Carver National Monument

5646 Carver Road
  Diamond, MO 64840
  (417) 325.4151

George Washington Carver National Monument is the birthplace and childhood home of the famed scientist, educator, and humanitarian. Established in 1943, it is the first unit of the National Park Service dedicated to Black Americans.

Bronze statue of young George Washington Carver

George Washington Carver Museum, Cultural, and Genealogical Center

1165 Angelina St
Austin, TX
(512) 974-4926

The Center is housed in a 36,000 square-foot facility with four galleries, a conference room, classroom, darkroom, dance studio, 134-seat theater, and archival space. In addition, there is a featured exhibit, *The African American Presence in 19th Century Texas.*

Harriet Tubman Museum and Cultural Center

424 Race Street
Cambridge, MD 21613-1836
(410)228-0401

The Harriet Tubman Museum & Educational Center is one of the oldest community organizations dedicated to the memory of Harriet Tubman. Inside the museum, visitors will find exhibits and resources. Volunteers answer questions and provide information on Harriet Tubman and the region; There are guided tours of local sites associated with Harriet Tubman available by appointment. In addition, the museum has a gift shop and brochures about area attractions.

PLACES TO VISIT

Harriet Tubman Underground Railroad National Monument and National Historical Park

4068 Golden Hill Road
Church Creek, MD 21622
(410)221-2290

The Harriet Tubman Underground Railroad National Historical Park is located in Maryland. Congress created it in December 2014. The park includes the Harriet Tubman Underground Railroad National Monument authorized by the United States president in 2013. The national historical park and the national monument are administered as a single unit, Harriet Tubman Underground Railroad National Historical Park, to recognize and interpret Harriet Tubman and the Underground Railroad.

Ida B. Wells-Barnett Museum and Cultural Center of African and African American History

220 North Randolph Street
Holly Springs, MS 38635
(662)252-3232
(662)579-5747 (To schedule a tour)

This museum is located in the Spires Bolling House, where Ida B. Wells and her parents were slaves. The home is included in the East Holly Springs Historic District and has been listed in the National Register of Historic Places since 1983. It became a Mississippi Landmark in 2000.

Ida B. Wells-Barnett Home

3624 S. Martin Luther King Jr. Blvd.
Chicago, IL 60653

It is located at 3624 S. Dr. Martin Luther King Jr. Drive in the Douglas community area of Chicago, Illinois. Civil rights advocate Ida B. Wells (1862–1931) and her husband Ferdinand Lee Barnett lived here from 1919 to 1930. It was listed on the National Register of Historic Places and as a National Historic Landmark on May 30, 1974. It was designated a Chicago Landmark on October 2, 1995.

Ids B. Wells-Barnett Home- Chicago

James Armistead Lafayette Casting

Lafayette Memorial
  Prospect Park
  Brooklyn, New York
  The Lafayette Memorial in Brooklyn was dedicated in 1917. It was based on the painting *Lafayette at Yorktown* of Gilbert du Motier, Marquis de Lafayette. Historians have identified James Armistead Lafayette with the Marquis, tending its horse wearing a military uniform, with a cockade and feather in his hat and cloak draped over his shoulders.

King Center

449 Auburn Avenue, NE
  Atlanta, Georgia 30312
  (404)526-8968
  Within the Martin Luther King, Jr. National Historical Park boundaries, the King family continues to honor the legacy of Rev. Dr. Martin Luther King, Jr and his wife, Honorable Coretta Scott King, with the King Center. Components include Dr. and Mrs. King's Crypt, The Eternal Flame, and Freedom Hall.

PLACES TO VISIT

The Tomb of Dr. Martin Luther King, Jr. and Coretta Scott King in Atlanta, Georgia

Major Dr. Martin Delany Memorial

Massie Creek Cemetery
  2077 Tarbox Cemetery Road
  Cedarville, Ohio
  The black granite memorial to the Delany family.

Major Martin R. Delany Exhibit

Heinz History Center
   1212 Smallman St.
   Pittsburgh, PA 15222
   (412)454-6000

A life-size figure of Major Dr. Delany and more information on his life's work is located in the Heinz History Center's featured exhibit *From Slavery to Freedom*. The long-standing display also includes a rare signed document from Delany.

Maj.Martin Delany exhibit- Heinz History Center

PLACES TO VISIT

Martin Luther King, Jr. National Historical Park

450 Auburn Avenue, NE.
Atlanta, GA
(404) 331-5190
Spread across 35 acres, the Martin Luther King, Jr. National Historical Park encompasses several buildings that were a part of the life and legacy of Rev. Dr. Martin Luther King, Jr., including his birth home and Ebeneezer Baptist Church.

Mary McLeod Bethune Council House

1318 Vermont Avenue NW
Washington, DC, 20005
(202) 673-2402
The Mary McLeod Bethune Council House National Historic Site illustrates the life and legacy of Mary McLeod Bethune. The house focuses on her career in Washington, DC, and her work and legacy of the National Council of Negro Women, Inc. (NCNW).

Mary McLeod Bethune Council House

PLACES TO VISIT

Minute Man National Historical Park

North Bridge / Park Head Quarters
174 Liberty St.
Concord, MA 01742
(978) 369-6993
Learn more about local Black Patriots and their contributions during the Revolutionary era at the Minute Man National Historical Park. The opening battles of the American Revolutionary War are brought to life as visitors explore the battlefields and structures associated with April 19, 1775, and witness the American revolutionary spirit through the writings of the Concord authors.

Monument to Bishop Richard Allen

Richard Allen Park
Grand River & West Chicago
Detroit, MI
Dedicated in July 1983 and created by Oscar Graves, this bronze tablet containing a round bronze relief with a bust of Bishop Richard Allen. The bronze tablet is mounted on a black granite base, facing Ebeneezer African Methodist Episcopal Church Detroit, Michigan.

Museum of African American History -two campuses

46 Joy Street
Boston, MA 02114
29 York Street
Five Corners
Nantucket, MA
(508)228.9833

The Museum of African American History is New England's largest museum dedicated to preserving, conserving, and interpreting the contributions of Black Americans. In Boston and Nantucket, the museum has held two historic sites and two Black Heritage Trails® that tell the story of organized Black communities from the Colonial Period through the 19th century. In Boston, the African Meeting House is the first of its kind in America and the oldest Back church building in the country. The adjacent Abiel Smith School is the oldest building in the nation constructed for the sole purpose of housing a Black public school. Today, the Abiel Smith School galleries feature rotating exhibits and a Museum Store open year-round.

On Nantucket Island, the Florence Higginbotham House sits next door to the pristinely restored African Meeting House. Visitors will find the African Meeting House open for scheduled hours during July and August and open by appointment at other times of the year.

Museum of the American Revolution

101 South Third Street
  Philadelphia, PA 19106
  (215) 253-6731

This museum has a copy of *Poems on Various Subjects, Religious and Moral*, written by Phillis Wheatley, the first published African-American author; this original copy of her work, published in 1773, is autographed by Wheatley.

National Afro-American Museum and Cultural Center

1350 Brush Row Road
  Wilberforce, Ohio 45384
  (937) 376-4944

PLACES TO VISIT

The National Afro-American Museum & Cultural Center opened to the public in April 1988. As a freshman at Central State University, our president, Dr. Arthur E. Thomas, mandated the entire student body, faculty, and staff to attend the ceremony. He also encouraged students to use it as an academic resource. The museum houses one of the United State's most extensive collections of Black American materials, including over 9,000 artifacts and artwork, 350 manuscript collections, and thousands of photographs.

National Afro-American History Museum and Cultural Center

National Memorial for Peace and Justice-Ida B. Wells Exhibit

417 Caroline Street
Montgomery, AL 36104
(334) 386-9100

The National Memorial for Peace and Justice, informally known as the National Lynching Memorial, is a national memorial to commemorate the Black victims of lynching in the United States. It includes a reflection space dedicated to Ida B. Wells, a selection of quotes by her, and a stone inscribed with her name.

National Museum of African American History and Culture

1400 Constitution Ave. NW,
Washington, DC 20560

The National Museum of African American History and Culture is a Smithsonian Institution museum located on the National Mall in Washington, DC, in the United States. It was established in December 2003 and opened its permanent home in September 2016 with a ceremony led by President Barack Obama.

Patriots of African Descent Monument

Valley Forge National Historical Park
1400 North Outer Line Drive
King of Prussia, PA 19406

The Patriots of African Descent Monument, located in the Valley Forge National Historic Park, was erected in 1993 by the Valley Forge Alumnae Chapter of Delta Sigma Theta Sorority, Inc. This monument is the first in a National Historical Park that honors the contributions made by the Black soldiers who fought during the American Revolutionary War and a tribute to those patriots who served during the Valley Forge encampment 1777-1778. The granite monument stands 9-foot-tall on Route 23.

Patriots of African Descent Monument

Reconstruction Era National Historical Park

706 Craven Street
Beaufort, SC 29902
Phone:
(843) 962-0039

The formerly called Reconstruction Era Monument was established in 2017. The John D. Dingell, Jr. Conservation, Management, and Recreation Act, signed in 2019, re-designated it as a National Historical Park. An exhibit dedicated to Robert Smalls is located here.

Richard Allen Cultural Center and Museum

412 Kiowa St
Leavenworth, KS 66048
(913) 682-8772
Richard Allen Cultural Center and Museum feature ruins of Bethel AME Church Underground Railroad site, artifacts from the Buffalo Soldiers, and memorabilia belonging to notable African-American figures such as General Colin Powell. The Center showcases bronze statues of Buffalo Soldiers and is home to the Everhard Collection, an exclusive Black Dignity photo gallery dating back to the late 1800s.

Robert Smalls Monument

Tabernacle Baptist Church Grounds
  907 South Craven Street
Beaufort, SC
  The Beaufort City Council erected the Robert Smalls statute in 1976.

Robert Smalls House

511 Prince Street
  Beaufort, SC, 29902.
  Robert Smalls purchased his former slave owner's house at a tax sale. After successfully winning a challenge to the sale (appealed to the US Supreme Court), the home remained in the family until 1953. It was designated a National Historic Landmark in 1974.

Texas African American History Memorial

100 West 11th Street
 Austin, Texas

Texas African American History Memorial Foundation erected the Texas African American History Memorial in 2016. Hendrick Arnold can be found in the casting.

Texas African American History Monument in Austin

Thurgood Marshall Memorial

Lawyers' Mall/State House Square
 State Circle

Annapolis, Maryland

The Thurgood Marshall Memorial was dedicated in 1996. An 8' statue of young Thurgood Marshall stands in front of pillars with the inscription "Equal Justice Under Law" facing two benches. It is in the location where the Maryland Court of Appeal heard Marshall winning arguments of the famous Murray case in 1935.

Tubman African American History Museum

310 Cherry Street
Macon, GA 31201
(478)743-8544

The Tubman Museum is the largest in the nation dedicated to educating people about the Art, History, and Culture of African Americans.

Wabash Avenue YMCA

3763 S. Wabash Avenue
Chicago, IL 60653
(773)924-9270

The Historic Former Wabash YMCA was the heart of cultural and economic progress for African Americans in the Bronzeville region of Chicago for over half a century and is hailed as the birthplace of Black History Month. It was listed on the U.S. National Register of Historic Places in 1986 and became a Chicago Landmark in 1998. The Renaissance Collaborative, Inc. (TRC) was founded in 1992 to restore and preserve the Historic Former Wabash Y. They host free on-site guided tours are offered on the 2nd and 4th Saturday of the month.

The Wabash YMCA in Chicago-birthplace of Black History Month

West End Museum - Prince and Primus Hall Exhibit

150 Lomasney Way,
  Boston, MA 02114
  Primus Hall exhibit
  The West End Museum, Inc. is a neighborhood museum in Boston, Massachusetts, in a 4000 square foot space on the ground floor of West End Place.

William Monroe Trotter House

National Historic Landmark
  97 Sawyer Avenue
  Boston, Massachusetts
  Home of African-American journalist and civil rights activist William Monroe Trotter. He and his wife Geraldine Louise Pindell moved into the two-story wood-frame home when they were married

in June 1899. William Monroe Trotter House was designated a National Historic Landmark and listed on the National Registrar of Historic Places 1976. In 1977, the exterior and the grounds were designated a Boston Landmark by the Boston Landmarks Commission. This house is not open to the public.

28

Commentary on Patriotism by Major Martin R. Delany

The following article was published in the North Star Newspaper in 1848. It has often been called Delany's "masterpiece".

Patriotism consists not in a mere professed love of country, the place of one's birth – an endearment to the scenery, however delightful and interesting, of such country; nor simply the laws and political policy by which such country is governed; but a pure and unsophisticated interest felt and manifested for man – an impartial love and desire for the promotion and elevation of every member of the body politic, their eligibility to all the rights and privileges of society. This, and other than this, fails to establish the claims of true patriotism.

From periods the most remote, the most improper application has been made of the endearing term Patriot. Whether the most absolute monarch, crowned with the hereditary diadem, armed with an unlimited sceptre, the most intolerable despot bearing the title of sovereign – the most cruel and heartless oppressor and slaveholder under the boasted title of President -the most relentless butcher and murderer called Commander-in-Chief – the most haughty and scornful aristocrat who tramples upon the people's rights in the halls of legislation – the most reckless and unprincipled statesman "rioting upon the spoils of a plundered revenue" – whether Phillips, Curran or Gratan in defence of Irish constitutional liberty – Emmet upon the scaffold, refusing to let his epitaph be written until Ireland was free - William Tell, under sentence of death, baffling the schemes of the German tyrant, Gesler – the French baron, Lafayette, leaving his native country and princely fortune, to share in common the fate of the struggling American Washington, as the leader of his country's destiny – O'Connell, as the Liberator – Thomas Jefferson, Patrick Henry, or John Quincy Adams, standing in the frontal ranks as defenders of American rights, or Mitchell and O'Brien, who sacrificed their all, being forever divorced and exiled from the most tender ties of domestic affections, by the severity of the laws of their country, for daring to discard provisions deemed pernicious to the welfare of their countrymen; all have laid equal claim to a share of the popular gratitude, and been endowed with the loved title of patriot.

A patriot may exist, whether blessed with the privileges of a country, favored with a free constituency, or flying before his pursuers, [and] roam an exile, the declared outlaw of the power that besets him. Love to man, and uncompromising hostility to that which interferes with his divine God-given rights, are the only traits which distinguish the true patriot. To be patriotic, is to be philanthropic; to be which, is necessary to love all men, regarding their humanity with equal importance.

Much has been the interest felt and manifested in this country in every movement, with exceptions to be named, whether home or abroad, in favor of human liberty, and those who were foremost in the struggle, bequeathed their names to present and future time, to become the subject of the poet and the theme of the historian. Spain, Italy, Greece, Poland, Germany, France,

COMMENTARY ON PATRIOTISM BY MAJOR MARTIN R. DELANY

England, Scotland and Ireland, of modern date, all, have had their patriots, each of whom in succession, has shared largely of America's eulogium. And of all who have scanned the ordeal before them, there were none perhaps for whom there has been expressed more sympathy, than the late victims of British displeasure, the Irish patriots and convicts, Mitchell and O'Brien, especially the latter, the severity of whose sentence aroused every feeling and expression of opposition to the execution of the sentence.

To witness the public demonstrations, as manifested in favor of the Irish struggle, in which Mayors of cities, Judges of Courts, sons of Ex-Presidents and Ex-Governors participated, and the universal interest felt in the result, is well tended to deceive, and betray into the idea those not otherwise advised, that this nation is a nation of justice. But how will America stand, when compared with other countries, dark as may be the gloom of their semi-barbarous laws? Condemned must she be in the moral vision of the whole enlightened world. Loud, long, and damning, must be the anathema uttered against her by those whom she treats and so regards in all her legal acknowledgments as aliens and enemies, ere their eyes be opened to a sense of their condition, and she still refuses to succor them.

But how many patriots have lived, toiled, suffered and died, having worn out a life of usefulness, unobtrusively laboring in the cause of suffering humanity, living to the community and the world a life of seclusion, passing to and fro unobserved, amidst the stir and busy scenes of a metropolis, and the throng and bustle of assembled thousands. This class of patriots may be found in every country, but to none are they more common than America, and in no country would they meet with less acceptance than in this Republic. Ever professing the most liberal principles, proclaiming liberty and equality to all mankind, their course of policy gives a glaring contradiction to their pretensions, and the lie to their professions.

Prone as they are to tyrannize and despotize over the liberties of the few, the philanthropist who espouses the cause of the oppressed, is destined to a life of obscurity; instead of commendation and renown, contempt and neglect are the certain and most bitter fruits of his reward. Marked and pointed out by the finger of scorn, he at once becomes the mock of the scoffer, and hiss of the reviler; and affliction heaped upon affliction presses upon him like a mountain weight, until at last he sinks under the mighty pressure, unable longer to bear it up. Yet, galling as this may be, it is a boon for which the downtrodden, oppressed American might anxiously long, compared with his own present miserable, unhappy condition.

Among them have existed, and there do exist, those who are justly entitled to all the claims of true patriotism; but proscription, as infamous as it is wicked, has stamped the seal of degradation upon their brow; and instead of patriots, they become the felon and outlaw. Anticipated and preconcerted by an inquisition of prejudice and slaveholding influence, the colored man of this confederacy, especially the bondman, is doomed to ignominy, whatever may be his merits.

Though he has complied with the first demand of a freeman – borne arms in defence of his country – no sooner is victory won, than he is unarmed, not only of his implements, but also of his equality with those among whom he bravely fought side by side for liberty and equality. Mathematician and philosopher he may be, not only furnishing to the country the only correct calendar of time and chronological cycles, but further contribute to its interest, by assisting in the plot and survey of the District of Columbia, without the aid of whose talents it could not at that time have been accomplished with mathematical accuracy; yet no sooner is this effected, than he is forgotten to the nation. Though in a professedly Republican and free Christian country, the yoke is upon his neck, and fetters upon his limbs, and dare he make the attempt to release himself and brethren from a

COMMENTARY ON PATRIOTISM BY MAJOR MARTIN R. DELANY

condition little less than death itself, the whole country is solemnly bound, in one confederated band, to riddle his breast with ten thousand balls. Is he a slave the most abject of South America or Cuba, who, rising in the majesty of his nature, with a bold and manly bearing, heads his enslaved brethren, leading them on to a holy contest for the liberty of their wives, mothers, sisters and children, he is, with one universal voice, denounced in this country, as a rebel, insurrectionist, cut-throat; and all the powers of despotism, America in the foremost rank, sallies forth in one united crusade against him.

Many are the untiring, uncompromising, stern and indefatigable enemies of oppression, and friends of God and humanity, now to be found among the nominally free colored people of this slavery-cursed land, at work laboring for the good of all men, though some have recently escaped from the American prison-house of bondage, bearing still fresh upon their quivering flesh the sting of the whip and marks of the lash, many of whom for talents and the qualified ability to write and speak, will favorably compare with the proudest despots and oppressors in the country.

Though they speak, act, petition, remonstrate, pray, and appeal, yet to all this the wickedness of the American people turns a deaf ear, and closed eye. Hence, the American colored patriot lives but to be despised, feared and hated, accordingly as his talents may place him in the community – moving amidst the masses, he passes unobserved, and at last goes down to the grave in obscurity, without a tear to condole his loss, or a breast to heave in sympathy. But the time shall yet come, when the name of the despised, neglected American patriot, in spite of American prejudice, shall rise superior to the spirit that would degrade it, and take its place on the records of merit and fame. M. R. D. (The North Star, 8 December 1848, P. 2).

29

References

We encourage you to read the books, articles, and visit the websites listed in this reference section to study more about these Great Black American Patriots.

Crispus Attucks

Cover photo of painting of Crispus Attucks. George Gaadt. Image available on the Internet and included in accordance with Title 17 U.S.C. Section 107. 25. Permission granted by artist. Retrieved online. 23 March 2021. http://www.gaadtstudio.com.

"Who is Crispus Attucks" *Crispus Attucks Museum*. Retrieved on-line . 23 March 2021. http://www.crispusattucksmuseum.org.

Photo of Crispus Attucks, the First Martyr of the American Revolution, King now State Street, Boston, March 5th. Image available on the Internet and included in accordance with Title 17 U.S.C. Section 107. 23. Retrieved online. 23 March 2021. http://www.loc.gov/item/2004676493/.

REFERENCES

Photo of portrait of Attucks. Artist unknown. Image available on the Internet and included in accordance with Title 17 U.S.C. Section 107. 25. Retrieved online. 23 March 2021. https://nypost.com/2020/05/23/this-memorial-day-our-heroes-show-us-values-worth-fighting-for/.

Benjamin Banneker

"Who was Benjamin Banneker?" *The Benjamin Banneker Foundation online.* 23 March 2021. https://www.bannekerfoundation.com/.

Photo of portrait of Benjamin Banneker. The Family of Benjamin Banneker. Image available on the Internet and included in accordance with Title 17 U.S.C. Section 107. 25. Retrieved online. 23 march 2021. https://about.usps.com/publications/pub354.pdf.

Photo of Benjamin Banneker on his almanac of the year 1795. Image available on the Internet and included in accordance with Title 17 U.S.C. Section 107. 25. Retrieved online from PBS. Author unknown. 23 March 2021. http://www.pbs.org/wgbh/aia/part2/2h68b.html.

Highsmith, Carol M, photographer. "Benjamin Banneker: Surveyor-Inventor-Astronomer," mural by Maxime Seelbinder, at the Recorder of Deeds building, 515 D St., NW, Washington, D.C. Photograph. Image available on the Internet and included in accordance with Title 17 U.S.C. Section 107. 25. Retrieved from the Library of Congress. 23 March 2021. www.loc.gov/item/2010641717/

Phillis Wheatley

"Who is Phillis Wheatley." *Phillis Wheatley Historical Society online.* 23 March 2021. http://www.phillis-wheatley.org/about-us/

Photo of portrait of Phillis Wheatley in *Revue des colonies. January 1837.* Author unknown. Retrieved online from PBS. Image available on the Internet and included in accordance with Title 17 U.S.C. Section 107. 25. *23 March 2021.* https://www.pbs.org/wgbh/aia/part2/2h77.html

Moorhead, Scipio, Active , Engraver. Phillis Wheatley, Negro servant to Mr. John Wheatley, of Boston. [London, Archd. Bell, Sept. 1] Photograph. Retrieved from the Library of Congress. Image available on the Internet and included in accordance with Title 17 U.S.C. Section 107. 25. 23 March 2021. www.loc.gov/item/2002712199/.

Photo of Letter to Phillis Wheatley from Gen. George Washington.George Washington Papers, Series 3, Varick Transcripts, 1775-1785, Subseries 3H, Personal Correspondence, 1775-1783, Letter book 1: May 31, 1775 - Dec. 25, 1779. Image available on the Internet and included in accordance with Title 17 U.S.C. Section 107. 25. Retrieved online. 23 March 2021. https://www.loc.gov/resource/mgw3h.001/?q=wheatley&sp=13&st=text

James Armistead Lafayette

The Unsung Heroes Project. Retrieved online. 23 March 2021. https://www.unsungheroesproject.com/about.html

"American Spies of the Revolution."*George Washington Mount Vernon website.* Retrieved online. 23 March 2021. https://www.mountverno

REFERENCES

n.org/george-washington/the-revolutionary-war/spying-and-espionage/american-spies-of-the-revolution/

"Engraved portrait of James Armistead Lafayette (c. 1759-1830)". After the painting by John B. Martin, ca. 1824.circa 1784.Cropped from image at Virginia Historical Society on the Library of Virginia website. Author unknown engraver, based on painting by John B. Martin.Retrieved online. 23 March 2021. https://www.lva.virginia.gov/public/archivesmonth/2005/vhs/VHS_4.htm

Schomburg Center for Research in Black Culture, Manuscripts, Archives and Rare Books Division, The New York Public Library. "Lafayette, James Armistead - Facsimile of the Marquis de Lafayette's original certificate commending James Armistead Lafayette for his revolutionary war service with portrait after John B. Martin." The New York Public Library Digital Collections. 1784.Retrieved online. 23 March 2021. https://digitalcollections.nypl.org/items/65de8e90-ff67-0133-5a69-00505686a51c

Dunsmore, John Ward. George Washington and Lafayette at Valley Forge. 1907. Retrieved on.ine. 23 March 2021. https://www.loc.gov/pictures/item/91792202/

Prince and Primus Hall

"Prince Hall Article" *The West End Museum online.* 23 March 2021. https://thewestendmuseum.org/article/prince-hall/.

"Primus Hall Article."*The West End Museum online.*23 March 2021. https://thewestendmuseum.org/article/primus-hall/

"Prince Hall -People of the Revolution - Free African-American Soldier and Mason." *History is Fun online.* 23 March 2021. https://www.historyisfun.org/learn/learning-center/prince-hall/

Scott Travis. "This Black Abolitionist Fought In The Revolutionary War With George Washington." *The Federalist.* Retrieved online. 23 March 2021. https://thefederalist.com/2017/02/15/black-abolitionist-fought-revolutionary-war-george-washington/

Photo of portrait of Prince Hall (c.1735 – December 4, 1807). Unknown date. Grand Logde of British Culumbia and Yukon[1] Author unknown. Retrieved online. 23 March 2021. http://freemasonry.bcy.ca/prince_hall/PrnceHll.jpg.Public domain.

Trumball, John. Photo of painting.The Surrender of General Burgoyne at Saratoga, October 16, 1777.typepainting. between circa 1822 and circa 1832. oil on canvas 53.7 cm (21.1 in): 77.8 cm (30.6 in). Yale University Art Gallery Blue pencil.svg.1832. Retrieved online. 23 March 2021. https://artgallery.yale.edu/collections/objects/113. Public domain.

McBarron, Jr., Hugh Charles. Photo of Battle of Trenton, a painting. July 1975. U.S. Army Center of Military History.Published by U.S. Government Printing Office; Retrieved online. 23 March 2021. https://history.army.mil/html/artphoto/pripos/prporevwar.html. Public domain.

Ranney, William (1813-1857). Photo of painting of The Battle of Cowpens. 1845. Blue pencil.svg. Retrieved online. 23 March 2021. https://www.nps.gov/cowp/learn/education/unit-7-the-battle-the-human-element.htm. Public domain.

Photo of The Battle of Harlem Heights, September 16, 1776. 1775. Printmaker Green, Valerie; Hall, Henry Brian; Longarce, James. Scaned by NYPL digital ID d5f662f0-c609-012f-8e8d-58d385a7bc34: Retrieved online.23 march 2021. https://digitalcollections.nypl.org/items/510d47da-2e92-a3d9-e040-e00a18064a99. Public domain.

Peter Salem and other Black Patriots

"Peter Salem biography" *America Battlefield Trust website. 26 March 2021.* https://www.battlefields.org/learn/biographies/peter-salem

White, Deborah Gray; Bay, Mia;Waldo E. Martin Jr. Freedom on My Mind: A History of African Americans A Black Patriot. Bedford/St. Martin's; First Edition 2016.

Greenwalt, Phillip S. George Washington's Integrated Army-The American Armies of the Revolution. Retrieved online.23 March 2021. https://www.battlefields.org/learn/articles/george-washingtons-integrated-army

Mofford, Juliet Haines, Andover Massachusetts: Historical Selections from Four Centuries. Retrieved online. 23March 2021. https://andoverhistorical.org/history-american-revolution

Nell, W.C. Colored Patriots" of New Hampshire.1855. Retrieved online. 23 March 2021. http://www.seacoastnh.com/colored-patriots-of-nh/?showall=1

Photo of portrait of Barzillai Lew. Unknown year. access online. 23 March 2021. https://fiftysevenacademics.tumblr.com/post/148713685955/hi-loved-your-post-about-18th-century-hair-care. Public domain.

Photo of 10 cent postage stamp depicting Salem Poor.1975.USPS. Author: United States Postal Service. Retrieved online.23 march 2021. https://commons.wikimedia.org/wiki/File:00SalemPoor.jpg

Phot0 of The Death of General Warren at the Battle of Bunker's Hill, June 17,1775. paintng. 1786. oil on canvas. Height: 50.1 cm (19.7 in); Width: 75.5 cm (29.7 in). Museum of Fine Arts Blue pencil.svg. 1977.853. United States of America. Retrieved online. 23 March 2021. http://www.mfa.org/collections/object/the-death-of-general-warren-at-the-battle-of-bunker-s-hill-17-june-1775-34260.

Photo of Peter Salem Home site."Handbook of Historical Data Concerning Leicester, Massachusetts"Access Genealogy website. Author Unknown. Retrieved online 1 August 2021. https://accessgenealogy.com/massachusetts/handbook-historical-data-concerning-leicester-massachusetts.htm

Bishop Richard Allen

McMickle,Marvin Andrew. An Encyclopedia of African American Christian Heritage.Judson Press. 2002. Retrieved online . 23 March 2021. https://aaregistry.org/story/richard-allen-bishop-ames-first-leader/

"Richard Allen, Bishop, AME Leader born." *African American Registry website*. Retrieved online.23 march 2021. https://aaregistry.org/story/richard-allen-bishop-ames-first-leader/

Photo of portrait of Richard Allen, a Methodist bishop and founder of the African Methodist Episcopal Church. 1891. Richard Allen, from the frontispiece of History of the African Methodist Episcopal Church (1891). Payne, Daniel. Retrieved online. 23 March 2021. https://aaregistry.org/story/richard-allen-bishop-ames-first-leader/

Photo of portrait of Absalom Jones by Raphaelle Peale. 1810. oil on paper mounted on board. Height: 30 in (76.2 cm); Width: 25 in (63.5 cm). Delaware Art Museum. Blue pencil.svg. Retrieved online. 23 March 2021. https://www.pabook.libraries.psu.edu/literary-cultural-heritage-map-pa/feature-articles/philadelphia-under-siege-yellow-fever-1793

Illustration of the Mother Bethel African Methodist Episcopal Church, the first American church for Black congregations founded by Richard Allen in Philadelphia, Pennsylvania, 1786. (Kean Collection/Getty Images). Retrieved online. 23 march 2021.

Harriet Tubman

Clark, Alexis. *After the Underground Railroad, Harriet Tubman Led a Brazen Civil War Raid. The History Channel online. Orginally published November 1, 2019.* Retrieved on 23 March 2021. https://www.history.com/news/harriet-tubman-combahee-ferry-raid-civil-war

Powelson, Benjamin F, photographer. Portrait of Harriet Tubman / Powelson, photographer, 77 Genesee St., Auburn, New York. [Auburn, N.Y.: Benjamin Powelson, or 1869] Photograph. Retrieved from the Library of Congress online. 23 March 2021.www.loc.gov-/item/2018645050/

Mcpherson & Oliver, photographer. 2nd South Carolina Infantry

Regiment raid on rice plantation, Combahee, South Carolina, and escaped slave named Gordon. New York: Harper's Weekly, July 4. Photograph. Retrieved from the Library of Congress online. 23 March 2021. www.loc.gov/item/2014645368/

Photo of Portrait of Harriet Tubman. circa. 1860-1880. Author unknown. Retrieved online. 23 March 2021. https://www.harriettubmanhome.com/

Frederick Douglass

Warren, George Kendall. Photo of portrait of Rev. Frederick Douglass gazing slightly off camera. circa 1879. National Archives and Records Administration. NAID 558770. DOD War and Conflict collection. Retrieved online. 23 Marchh 2021. https://www.archives.gov/exhibits/documented-rights/exhibit/section2/detail/frederick-douglass.html

Boxill, B.R. Frederick Douglass's Patriotism. *J Ethics* 13, 301 (2009). https://doi.org/10.1007/s10892-009-9067-x

Great American Patriot Frederick Douglass. USA Patriotism! website. Retrieved 21 March 2021. https://www.usapatriotism.org/gap/douglass_f.htm

Photograph of Anna Murray Douglass (1813–1882), the first wife of Frederick Douglass. Photograph first published in Rosetta Douglass Sprague, "My Mother As I Recall Her", 1900 -. Retrieved online 23 March 2021. http://memory.loc.gov/mss/mfd/02/02007/0002.jpg

Photo of Retouched portrait of Frederick Douglass taken in the

REFERENCES

1840s.Unknown author - Retrieved online. 23 March 2021. http://explorepahistory.com/displayimage.php?imgId=1619

Photo of Frederick Douglass reading FRDO 3899. Image available on the Internet and included in accordance with Title 17 U.S.C. Section 107. Retrieved online. 23 March 2021. https://www.nps.gov/media/photo/gallery.htm?pg=2813693&id=3020ED03-1DD8-B71C-07C2C1EA7AD31EF7

Composite of several images of Frederick Douglass. 1840s thru 1890s. Wikimedia Commons. Various author.Retrieved online. 23 March 2021. https://commons.wikimedia.org/wiki/File:Frederick_Douglass_composite.png

Rober Smalls

"Robert Smalls biography". *National Park Services website*. Retrieved online. 23 March 2021. https://www.nps.gov/people/robert-smalls.htm

"Did You Know... Former Slave Bought His Master's House and Served as a Collector of Customs?"*U.S. Custom and Border Patrol Website*. Retrieved online. 21 June 2021. https://www.cbp.gov/about/history/did-you-know/collector-customs

"Smalls, Robert". *History, Art,& Archives United States House of Representatives*. Retrieved online. 21 June 2021. https://history.house.gov/People/Detail/21764

Photo of picture of Robert Smalls. 14 June 1862. Author unknown. Retrieved online. 21 May 2021. http://www.sonofthesouth.net/leefo

undation/civil-war/1862/june/robert-smalls-planter.htm

Photo of images of the Planter's crew adapted from "Heroes in Ebony–The captors of the Rebel steamer Planter, Robert Small, W. Morrison, A. Gradine and John Small," Frank Leslie's Illustrated Newspaper, June 21m 1862, via Library of Congress. Retrieved online. 23 March 2021. https://www.loc.gov/pictures/item/99403228/

Photo of Robert Smalls, captain of the gun-boat "Planter" The gun-boat "Planter," run out of Charleston, S.C., by Robert Smalls, May. Photograph. Retrieved from the Library of Congress. Retrieved online. 23 March 2021. www.loc.gov/item/97512451/.

Photo of Robert Smalls. Library of Congress description: "Robert Smalls, S.C. M.C. Born in Beaufort, SC, April 1839". Between 1870 and 1880. Mathew Brady (1822–1896) Levin Corbin Handy (1855–1932) Restored by Adam Cuerden. Retrieved online. 23 March 2021. https://www.nps.gov/people/robert-smalls.htm

Major Dr. Alexander T. Augusta

Buckley, Gail Lumet. American Patriots: The Story of Blacks in the Military from the Revolution to Desert Storm. Random House Trade Paperbacks. 2002.

"Binding Wounds, Pushing Boundaries: African Americans in Civil War Medicine exhibition" U.S. National Library of Medicine. Retrieved online. 19 March 2021. https://www.nlm.nih.gov/exhibition/bindingwounds/inuniform.html

Newmark, Jill L. "A Civil War Surgeon Book Rediscovered". *U.S.*

REFERENCES

National Library of Medicine. April 4, 2014. https://circulatingnow.nl m.nih.gov/2014/04/04/a-civil-war-surgeons-books-rediscovered/

Photo of Howard University Medical Department, Agusta on far right. Publication date and author unknown. Image available on the Internet and included with the Title 17 U.S.C. Section 107 Retrieved online. 23 March 2021. http://circulatingnow.nlm.nih.gov/2014/04/04/a-civil-war-surgeons-books-rediscovered/

Photo of Major Dr. Alexander Agusta. Publication date and author unknown. Image available on the Internet and included with the Titile 17 U.S.C Section 107. Retrieved online 23 March 2021. https://magazine.utoronto.ca/campus/history/doctor-of-courage-alexander-augusta-civil-rights-hero/

Photo of Jan 7, 1863: Letter from Dr. Augusta to President Lincoln. Photo: National Archives and Records Administration. https://www.archives.gov/research/african-americans/slavery-records-civil.html

Taylor, Alice. "Doctor of Courage". *The University of Toronoto Magazine.* February 3, 2015. Retrieved online. 23march 2021. https://magazine.utoronto.ca/campus/history/doctor-of-courage-alexander-augusta-civil-rights-hero/

Photo of Lithograph of Campbell Army Hospital, later known as Freedmen's Hospital. c. 1864. published by Magnus, Charles.Courtesy Historical Society of Washington, D.C. Retrieved online. 23 March 2021. https://www.nlm.nih.gov/exhibition/bindingwounds/within.html

Photo of Grave monument for Dr. Alexander Thomas Augusta and his family at Arlington National Cemetery. Courtsey of Arlington National Cemetery. Publish date and author unknown. Retrieved online. *24 March 2021.* https://www.nps.gov/foth/learn/historycultu re/alexander-augusta.htm

Greenbury Logan

Schoen, Harold . "The Free Negro in the Republic of Texas, II" The Southwestern Historical Quarterly. Vol. 40.No.1. (Jul., 1936), Texas State Historical Association. Retrieved online. 21 June 2021. https://www.jstor.org/stable/30235596

Katz, William Loren. The Black West: A Documentary and Pictorial History of the African American Role in the Westward Expansion of the United States.Harlem Moon/Broadway Books. 2002.

Photo of Portrait of Greenbury Logan. Image available on the Internet and included in accordance with Title 17 U.S.C Section 107. Publish date and author unknown. Retrived online. 21 March 2021. http://www.brookelandisd.net/page/open/3465/0/Chapter%2013% 20Section%201%20Reading.pdf

Photo of painting of Greenburry Logan at the Battle of San Jacinto. Image available on the Internet and included in accordance with Title 17 U.S.C. Section 107. Publish date and author unknown. Retrieved online. 21 March 2021. https://internetlooks.com/historyoftexas.ht ml

Photo of painting of Hendrick Arnold and Greenbury Logan at the Siege of Bexar. c. 1975. Emanuel, Milton. General Photograph Collection. 075-0679. Retrieved online. 21 march 2021. https://digit

REFERENCES

al.utsa.edu/digital/collection/p9020coll008/id/9581/

Hendrick Arnold

Thompson, Nolan. "Hendrick Arnold (unknown-1849)".*Texas State Historical Association Handbook of Texas*. Retrieved online. 23 March 2021. https://www.tshaonline.org/handbook/entries/arnold-hendrick.

Schoen, Harold . "The Free Negro in the Republic of Texas, II" The Southwestern Historical Quarterly. Vol. 40.No.1. (Jul., 1936), Texas State Historical Association. Retrieved online. 21 June 2021. https://www.jstor.org/stable/30235596

Photo of painting of Hendrick Arnold standing beside a horse. Joseph Randolph. Publish date unknown. Texas Southern University. 068-1103. General photograph collection. Image available on the Internet and included in accordance with Title 17 U.S.C. Section 107.Retrieved online. 21 March 2021. https://digital.utsa.edu/digital/collection/p9020coll008/id/5943/

Photo of painting of Siege of Bexar. Image available on the Internet and included in accordance with Title 17 U.S.C. Section 107. Publish date and author Emanuel Milton. Retrieved online 23 March 2021. https://www.sutori.com/item/the-siege-of-bexar-october-12-1835-over-the-course-of-multiple-weeks-the-a-tex

Photo of paintng of Painting of Hendrick Arnold and Greenbury Logan at the Siege of Bexar in December 1835. Author M.A. Emanuel. Texas Southern University. 068-1101. General Photograph collection. . Image available on the Internet and included in accordance with Title 17 U.S.C. Section 107. Retrieved online 23 March 2021. https://digit

al.utsa.edu/digital/collection/p9020coll008/id/5946/rec/2

Major Martin Delaney

Sterling, Dorothy. The Making of an Afro-America : Martin Robison Delany, 1812-1885 .Da Capo Press (August 22, 1996).

Surkamp,Jim. "True Patriotism"-Martin Delaney "Masterpiece". 28 December 2011. Retrieved online. 23 March 2021. https://myshepherdstown.wordpress.com/tag/ireland/

Levine, Robert S. "Martin Delany, Frederick Douglass and the Politics of Representative Identity," University of North Carolina Press, 1997. Print.

Photo of painting of Martin Delaney in Uniform. National Portrait Gallery.Stanford, Eleanor. Image available on the Internet and included in accordance with Title 17 U.S.C. Section 107. Retrieved online 23 March 2021. https://www.si.edu/exhibitions/bound-freedoms-light-african-americans-and-civil-war-event-exhib-4702

Photo of Major Martin Delaney in Milatary Uniform. Image available on the Internet and included in accordance with Title 17 U.S.C. Section 107. Retrieved online 23 March 2021. https://www.post-gazette.com/local/pittsburgh-history/2014/02/02/Respected-black-editor-endured-mistreatment/stories/201402020089

Photo of original grave maker for Maj. Martin Delany (name misspelled). Image available on the Internet and included with Title 17 U.S.C. Section 107. Retrieve 23 March 2021. http://lestweforget.hamptonu.edu/page.cfm?uuid=9FEC3551-A102-FDE4-4E1D667C01

REFERENCES

02A65C

Mary McLeod Bethune

Howard. Spencer. "Bethune: Advisor to the President". *National Archives Hoover Heads.* February 3, 2021. Retrieved online 21 June 2021. https://hoover.blogs.archives.gov/2021/02/03/mary-bethune-adviser-to-presidents/

"The Extraordinary Life of Mary McLeod Bethune". *The National WWII Museum. Retrieved 22 March 2021.* https://www.nationalww2museum.org/war/articles/mary-mcleod-bethune

McCluskey, Audrey Thomas and Elaine M. Smith. *Mary McLeod Bethune: Building a Better World.* Indiana University Press, 1999.

Long, Nancy Ann Zrinyi. *Mary McLeod Bethune: Her Life and Legacy.* Florida Historical Society Press, 2019.

Photo of *Mary McLeod Bethune with students at the Daytona Educational and Industrial School for Negro Grils. c. 1905. Image from State Archives of Florida, Florida Memory.* Image available on the Internet and included in accordance with Title 17 U.S.C. Section 107. Retrieved 20 March 2021. https://www.nationalww2museum.org/war/articles/mary-mcleod-bethune

Photo of *Mary McLeod Bethune, Daytona Beach, 1915. Image from State Archives of Florida, Florida Memory.* Image available on the Internet and included in accordance with Title 17 U.S.C. Section 107. Retrieved 20 March 2021. https://www.nationalww2museum.org/war/articles/mary-mcleod-bethune

Photo of *Mary McLeod Bethune, Director of NYA Negro Affairs, 1943. Image from Library of Congress, 2017843211.* Image available on the Internet and included in accordance with Title 17 U.S.C. Section 107. Retrieved 20 March 2021. https://www.nationalww2museum.org/war/articles/mary-mcleod-bethune

Photo of *Mary McLeod Bethune in WAND uniform, 1944. Image from Tuskegee University Archives.* Image available on the Internet and included in accordance with Title 17 U.S.C. Section 107. Retrieved 20 March 2021. https://www.nationalww2museum.org/war/articles/mary-mcleod-bethune

Photo of *Mary McLeod Bethune in 1949. Image from Library of Congress, 2004662601.* Image available on the Internet and included in accordance with Title 17 U.S.C. Section 107. Retrieved 20 March 2021. https://www.nationalww2museum.org/war/articles/mary-mcleod-bethune

Monroe Trotter

Asante, Molefi Kete; Mattson, Mark T. The African-American atlas : Black history and culture—an illustrated reference New York.Macmillan. revised 1991.

Portrait of Monroe Trotter. Artist Larry Johnson. Medium Oil. Dimensions Approx. 20 x 27 in. Date. 1991. Image available on the Internet and included in accordance with Title 17 U.S.C. Section 107. Retrieved online 25 Mach 2021. https://vc.bridgew.edu/hoba/index.html

Photo of The Guardian, A Boston newspaper founded by William

Monroe Trotter. This issue is dated August 30, 1902. –The Guardian August 1902. Image available on the Internet and included in accordance with Title 17 U.S.C. Section 107. Retrieved online 25 Mach 2021. https://www.boston.com/news/local-news/2016/04/26/new-boston-weekly-comes-under-fire-after-taking-name-of-former-african-american-newspaper

Photo of William Monroe Trotter, editor and founder of The Guardian.Photo courtesy of Joseph Nelson. Image available on the Internet and included in accordance with Title 17 U.S.C. Section 107. 25 March 2021. https://www.boston.com/news/local-news/2016/04/26/new-boston-weekly-comes-under-fire-after-taking-name-of-former-african-american-newspaper

W.E.B. DuBois

The Civil Rights Act of 1964: A Long Struggle for Freedom W. E. B. DuBois: A Recorded Autobiography". *Library of Congress. Retrieved online. 24 March 2021.* https://www.loc.gov/exhibits/civil-rights-act/multimedia/w-e-b-du-bois.html

"About W.E.B. DuBois" *W.E.B.DuBois National Historic Site. Retrieved online. 26 March 2021.* https://www.duboisnhs.org/about/

Photo of W. E. B. DuBois, photo taken in summer 1907 in connection with the annual Niagara Movement meeting. 1907. Author unknown. Image available on the Internet and included in accordance with Title 17 U.S.C. Section 107. Retrieved online 25 Mach 2021. http://www.library.umass.edu/spcoll/collections/galleries/dubois/MS0312-0408.jpg

Photo of Niagara movement meeting in Fort Erie, Canada, 1905. Author unknown. Image available on the Internet and included in accordance with Title 17 U.S.C. Section 107. Retrieved online 25 Mach 2021. https://www.loc.gov/exhibits/naacp/prelude.html

Photo of DuBois, W. E. B., Harvard graduation (dup.), 1890. Author unknown. Image available on the Internet and included in accordance with Title 17 U.S.C. Section 107. Retrieved online 25 Mach 2021. http://www.library.umass.edu/spcoll/collections/galleries/dubois/MS0312-0381.jpg

Photo of W.E.B. DuBois, half-length portrait, facing front. [Between 1930 and 1940] Retrieved from the Library of Congress, www.loc.gov-/item/95519694/

Dr. Charles Drew

"Charles Drew House" *Nation Parks Service. Last updated August 17, 2018. Retrieved online. 26 March 2021.* https://www.nps.gov/places/charles-drew-house.htm

Love, Spencie. *One Blood: The Death and Resurrection of Charles R. Drew.* Chapel Hill, NC: The University of North Carolina, 1996.

"Charles R. Drew". *U.S. National Library of Medicine Profiles in Science. Retrieved online 26 March 2021.* https://profiles.nlm.nih.gov/spotlight/bg/feature/biographical-overview

"Charles Drew: Unassuming hero of World War II". *Healio News. Hematology/Oncology. June 28, 2008. Retrieved online. 26 March 2021.* https://www.healio.com/news/hematology-oncology/20120325/ch

REFERENCES

arles-drew-unassuming-hero-of-world-war-ii

Photo of Dr. Charle Drew. Pubish date and author unknown. Image available on the Internet and included in accordance with Title 17 U.S.C. Section 107. Retrieved online 25 Mach 2021. https://profiles.nlm.nih.gov/spotlight/bg

United States Office Of War Information. Smith, Roger. Office of Civilian Defense worker help protect nation's capital. Demonstrating treatment of air-raid victim, medical corps officers instruct nurses in practice raid in Washington, D.C. This photo shows the Howard University medical unit headed by Dr. Charles Drew, which has been rated one of the country's finest. Apr. Photograph. Retrieved from the Library of Congress 22 June 2021 www.loc.gov/item/2017697572/.

Photo of Plasma transfer pack and extractor apparatus. The National Library of Medicine. 10149010. NLMID A030320. Image available on the Internet and included in accordance with Title 17 U.S.C. Section 107. Retrieved online 25 Mach 2021. https://collections.nlm.nih.gov/catalog/nlm:nlmuid-101449010-img

Ida B Wells

"Ida B Wells." Norwood, Arlisha. 2017. *National Women History Museum website*. Accessed online 31 July 2021. https://www.womenshistory.org/education-resources/biographies/ida-b-wells-barnett

Railton, Ben."Considering History: Women Whose Critical Patriotism Made America Better"The Saturday Evening Post. March 1,2021. Retrieved online. 28 march 2021. https://www.saturdayeveningpost.com/2021/03/considering-history-women-whose-critical-patriotis m-made-america-better/

Hudson Jr, David, L. "A Tribute to Ida B Wells and the Power of the Pen." Freedom Forum Institute. January 5, 2018. etrieved online. 29 March 2021. https://www.freedomforuminstitute.org/2018/01/05/a-tribute-to-ida-b-wells-and-the-power-of-the-pen/

Photo of Portrait of Ida B. Wells-Barnett. Publish date and author unknown. Image available on the Internet and included in accordance with Title 17 U.S.C. Section 107. Retrieved online. 29 March 2021. https://quotesgram.com/ida-b-wells-quotes/

Photo of Ida B. Wells. c 1893. Garrity,Mary. Image available on the Internet and included in accordance with Title 17 U.S.C. Section 107. Retrieved 28 March 2021. https://commons.wikimedia.org/wiki/File:Mary_Garrity_-_Ida_B._Wells-Barnett_-_Google_Art_Project_crop.jpg

Photo of Ida B. Wells-Barnett (1862–1931), wearing "Martyred Negro Soldiers" button, between 1917–1919. Facsimile. Ida B. Wells Papers, Special Collections Research Center, University of Chicago Library (061.03.00)]Retrieved online. 29 march 2021.https://www.loc.gov/exhibitions/women-fight-for-the-vote/about-this-exhibition/new-tactics-for-a-new-generation-1890-1915/new-tactics-and-renewed-confrontation/ida-b-wells-barnett-holds-her-ground/

Photo of Ida B. Wells-Barnett with her children Charles, Herman, Ida, and Alfreda. 1909. Author unknown. Image available on the Internet and included in accordance with Title 17 U.S.C. Section 107. Retrieved online 25 Mach 2021. https://www.lib.uchicago.edu/e/scrc/findingaids/view.phpeadid=ICU.SPCL.IBWELLS#idp84886768

REFERENCES

Booker T. Washington

Booker T Washington. The African American Desk Reference. Schomburg Center for Research in Black Culture, The Stonesong Press Inc. and The New York Public Library, John Wiley & Son Inc. Publishing. 1999.

Harlan, Louis R, ed., *The Booker T. Washington Papers*, Vol. 3, (Urbana: University of Illinois Press, 1974), 583–587.

Bain News Service, Publisher. Booker T. Washington. [No Date Recorded on Caption Card] Photograph. Retrieved from the Library of Congress. 29 march 2021. www.loc.gov/item/2014685040/.

Photo of Booker T Washington speaks to a large crowd during his last pilgrimage in Louisiana. c 1915. Arthur P. Bedou/Robert Abbott Sengstacke.Image available on the Internet and included in accordance with Title 17 U.S.C. Section 107. Retrieve online. 29 March 2021. https://publicdomainclip-art.blogspot.com/2006_02_01_archive.html

Booker T. Washington, half-length portrait, seated at desk[Between 1890 and 1910] Photograph. Retrieved from the Library of Congress .Image available on the Internet and included in accordance with Title 17 U.S.C. Section 107. Retrieve online. 29 March 2021. <www.loc.gov/item/98500608/>.

Photo of Map created by the Julius Rosenwald Fund shows the location of the schools throughout the southern states. Image courtesy of Fisk University, John Hope and Aurelia E. Franklin Library. Image available on the Internet and included in accordance with Title 17

U.S.C. Section 107. Retrieve online. 29 March 2021. https://www.ab hmuseum.org/the-rosenwald-schools-an-impressive-legacy-of-black-jewish-collaboration-for-negro-education/

George Washington Carver

Bolton, Sarah Knowles. *Lives of Poor Boys Who Became Famous.* Thomas Y Cromwell. New York. 1925, 1962.

Bontemps, Arna Wendell. *The Story of George Washington Carver.* Grossetnand Dunlap. New York. 1954

Maranzani, Barbara. "George Washington Carver's Powerful Circle of Friends"*Biography online.* Updated JAN 28, 2021. Original: JAN 14, 2019. Retrieved online. 29 March 2021. https://www.biography.com/news/george-washington-carver-friends

Portrait of George Washington Carver. Image available on the Internet and included in accordance with Title 17 U.S.C. Section 107. Retrieved online. 29 march 2021. https://science.howstuffworks.com/innovation/famous-inventors/george-washington-carvers-inventions.htm

Photo of Dr. George Washington Carver. Rothstein, Arthur. Tuskegee Institute, Alabama. . Retrieved from the Library of Congress. Image available on the Internet and included in accordance with Title 17 U.S.C. Section 107. Retrieve online. 29 March 2021. <www.loc.gov/item/2017828725/>.

Photo of George Washington Carver, full-length portrait, seated on steps, facing front, with staff. Johnston, Frances Benjamin. Retrieved

REFERENCES

from the Library of Congress. Image available on the Internet and included in accordance with Title 17 U.S.C. Section 107. Retrieve online. 29 March 2021<www.loc.gov/item/2004671560/>.

Photo of George Washington Carver shaking hands with President Roosevelt. Image available on the Internet and included in accordance with Title 17 U.S.C. Section 107. Retrieved online.29 march 2021. https://www.history.com/topics/black-history/george-washington-carver

Photo of Dr. George Washington Carver with Henry Ford after being presented with a modern, fully equipped laboratory for food research, a gift from Mr. Ford. Bettman. Image available on the Internet and included in accordance with Title 17 U.S.C. Section 107. Retrieved online. 29 march 2021 https://www.history.com/topics/black-history/george-washington-carver

Dr. Daniel Hale Williams

"Daniel Hale Williams Biography". *Biography*. Updated January 7,2021. Retrieved online 30 March 2021. https://www.biography.com/scientist/daniel-halennsavan

"Daniel Hale Williams: Marking Time". *Pennsylvania Heritage Magazine Online. Winter Issue 2010*. Retrieved online 30 March 2021. https://paheritage.wpengine.com/article/daniel-hale-williams-1856-1931/

Photo of Dr. Daniel Hale Williams c. 1900. Publish date and author unknown. Image available on the Internet and included in accordance with Title 17 U.S.C. Section 107. Retrieved online. 30 March 2021. https://www.biography.com/.image/t_share/MTE5NDg0MDU1M

TY2NDIwNDk1/daniel-hale-williams-wc-9532269-1-402.jpg

Photo of head and shoulders, full face image of Daniel Williams. Date unknown. Image available on the Internet and included in accordance with Title 17 U.S.C. Section 107. Retrieved online. 30 March 2021. https://collections.nlm.nih.gov/catalog/nlm:nlmuid-101448033-img

An undated photograph of nurses in front of Provident Hospital at its second location at 36th and Dearborn Streets, Chicago. CHM, ICHi-040212.Courtesy of Chicago History Museum. Retrieved online. https://www.chicagohistory.org/the-black-nurses-of-provident-hospital/

Thurgood Marshall

Gewirtz, Paul. "Thurgood Marshall." *The Yale Law Journal*, vol. 101, no. 1, 1991, pp. 13–18. *JSTOR*, www.jstor.org/stable/796932. Accessed 22 March 2021.

Vasillopulos, Christopher. "Prevailing Upon the American Dream: Thurgood Marshall and Brown v. Board of Education." *The Journal of Negro Education*, vol. 63, no. 3, 1994, pp. 289–296. *JSTOR*, www.jstor.org/stable/2967181. Accessed 23 March 2021.

The Reader's Companion to American History. Eric Foner and John A. Garraty, Editors. Copyright © 1991 by Houghton Mifflin Harcourt Publishing Company. All rights reserved.

Photograph of Thurgood Marshall. between 1935-1940. Author unknown. Tribune.November 23,1946. Library of Congress. Image available on the Internet and included in accordance with Title 17

REFERENCES

U.S.C. Section 107. Retrieved online. 30 March 2021. https://www.loc.gov/item/95519435/

Photo of George Edward Chalmer Hayes, Thurgood Marshall, and James Nabrit Jr. in 1954 winning Brown case. 1954. New York World-Telegram & Sun Collection at LOC. Author unknown. Image available on the Internet and included in accordance with Title 17 U.S.C. Section 107. Retrieved online. 30 March 2021. https://www.washingtonpost.com/opinions/2021/05/17/lets-pause-mark-brown-v-board-education-its-lessons-our-time/

Photo of Thurgood Marshall. 1967. Okamoto, Yoichi R. National Archives and Record Administration.2803441. Image available on the Internet and included in accordance with Title 17 U.S.C. Section 107. Retrieved online. 30 March 2021. https://catalog.archives.gov/id/2803441

Dr. Ben Carson

"Ben Carson Biography". *Biography*. Origianaly published April 2, 2014. Updated January 11, 2021. Retrieved online. 30 March 2021.

Photo of Young Ben Carson. Publish date and author unknown. Image available on the Internet and included in accordance with Title 17 U.S.C. Section 107. Retrieved online. 30 March 2021. https://bencarson-neurosurgeon-moesha.weebly.com/ben-carson-childhood.html

Photo of Ben Carson with a Johns Hopkins surgical team in an undated photo. Johns Hopkins Medicine. Image available on the Internet and included in accordance with Title 17 U.S.C. Section 107. Retrieved online. 30 March 2021. https://www.nytimes.com/2015/11/23/us/

politics/with-ben-carson-the-doctor-and-the-politician-can-vary-sh arply.html?WT.nav=top-news&action=click&clickSource=story-hea ding&hp&module=photo-spot-region&pgtype=Homepage&region= top-news

Photo Dr. Ben Carson. Official potrial as HUD secretary. 20 April 2017. United StatesDpartment of Housing and Urban Development. . Image available on the Internet and included in accordance with Title 17 U.S.C. Section 107. Retrieved online. 30 March 2021. https://mo bile.twitter.com/SecretaryCarson/photo

Rev. Dr.Martin Luther King, Jr.

"How Dr.King cited the Constitution in his Mountaintop Speech". *National Contitution Center website.* January 15, 2018. Retrieved online. 30 March 2021. https://constitutioncenter.org/blog/how-dr-king-ci ted-the-constitution-in-his-mountaintop-speech/

Portrait of Rev. Dr. Martin Luther King, Jr. Image available on the Internet and included in accordance with Title 17 U.S.C. Section 107. Retrieved online. 30 March 2021. http://www.jsonline.com/news/e ducation/an-act-of-hate-results-in-a-positive-solution-b99186610z 1-240897991.html

Photo of Martin Luther King, Jr. leaves the West Wing after meeting with President Johnson. August 5, 1965. Abbie Rowe, NPS: National Archive and Records Administration. Image available on the Internet and included in accordance with Title 17 U.S.C. Section 107. Re trieved online. 30 March 2021. https://obamawhitehouse.archives.g ov/blog/2012/01/16/archives-dr-martin-luther-king-white-house

REFERENCES

Photo of President Lyndon B. Johnson meets with Civil Rights leaders Martin Luther King, Jr., Whitney Young, and James Farmer in the Oval Office. January 18, 1964. Image available on the Internet and included in accordance with Title 17 U.S.C. Section 107. Retrievedonline. 30 March 2021. https://prologue.blogs.archives.gov/2018/02/28/lbj-and-mlk/

Photo of Dr. King at Mason Temple. 1968. Vernon Matthews. The Commericial Appeal. Image available on the Internet and included in accordance with Title 17 U.S.C. Section 107. Retrieved online. 30 March 2021. https://www.gannett-cdn.com/presto/2021/02/03/USAT/4e2d8a9e-5bc5-41bd-81d5-c14f4ddd5b8b-USP_News__Sanitation_Strike_Marches.jpg

Dr. Carter G. Woodson

"Carter G. Woodson". *National Park Services website. Last updated may 2, 2021. Retrieved online. 30 March 2021.*

Lankford, Reign. The Origin of Black History Month. *The Pat Post.* March 1, 2021. https://patriot-post.com/features/2021/03/01/the-origins-of-black-history-month/

Portrait of Dr. Carter G. Woodson, Image available on the Internet and included in accordance with Title 17 U.S.C. Section 107. https://www.africanamericanhistorymonth.gov/collections.html

Woodson at work in his study, circa 1940s. (Photo: Scurlock Studio Records, ca. 1905-1994, Archives Center, National Museum of American History)

Mary McLeod Bethune, Lucy Harth Smith, and Dr. Carter G. Woodson at ASALH's Annual Conference in Chicago, Illinois in 1940. Bethune-Cookman University, Mary McLeod Bethune Foundation National Historic Landmark

Places to visit

Photo of African American Civil War Memorial. Image available on the Internet and included in accordance with Title 17 U.S.C. Section 107. 23. Retrieved online. 27 May 2021. https://www.doi.gov/blog/defining-moments-and-historic-places-civil-war

Photo of Benjamin Banneker and the Boundary Stones of the District of Columbia. Image available on the Internet and included in accordance with Title 17 U.S.C. Section 107. 23. Retrieved online. 27 May 2021. https://www.nps.gov/places/sw-9-intermediate-boundary-stone-of-the-district-of-columbia.htm

Photo of Boston Massacre/Crispus Attucks Monument. Malarkey83. 14 March 2008. . Image available on the Internet and included in accordance with Title 17 U.S.C. Section 107. 23. Retrieved online. 27 March 2021. https://web.archive.org/web/20161013181811/http://www.panoramio.com/photo/22933938

Photo of Charles Richard Drew Memorial Marker, Haw River. Jordan, Patrick. May 2010. Courtesy of HMdb.org.Image available on the Internet and included in accordance with Title 17 U.S.C. Section 107. 23. Retrieved online. 27 March 2021. https://docsouth.unc.edu/commland/monument/165/

Photo of Young George Washington Carver. Image available on the

REFERENCES

Internet and included in accordance with Title 17 U.S.C. Section 107. 23. Retrieved online. 27 March 2021. https://www.nps.gov/articles/000/plan-like-a-park-ranger-top-10-tips-for-visiting-george-washington-carver-nm.htm

Photo of Ida B. Wells-Barnett Home. Image available on the Internet and included in accordance with Title 17 U.S.C. Section 107. 23. Retrieved online. 27 March 2021. https://commons.wikimedia.org/wiki/File:20070601_Wells_House_(2).JPG

Photo of The Tomb of Dr. Martin Luther King, Jr. and Coretta Scott King in Atlanta, Georgia. Fairbanks, Mike. 12 Dec 2012. Image available on the Internet and included in accordance with Title 17 U.S.C. Section 107. 23. Retrieved online. 27 March 2021. https://commons.wikimedia.org/wiki/File:The_Tomb_of_Dr._Martin_Luther_King,_Jr._and_Coretta_Scott_King_in_Atlanta,_Georgia.jpg

Photo of Patriots of African Descent Monument. Image available on the Internet and included in accordance with Title 17 U.S.C. Section 107. 23. Retrieved online. 27 March 2021.https://www.nps.gov/vafo/learn/historyculture/africanpatriotsmonument.htm

Photo of Major Martin Delany exhibit. O'neil, Annie. Image available on the Internet and included in accordance with Title 17 U.S.C. Section 107. 23. Retrieved online. 27 March 2021. https://www.heinzhistorycenter.org/exhibits/from-slavery-to-freedom

Photo of the Wabash YMCA. Jameson, Andrew. 29 August 2010. mage available on the Internet and included in accordance with Title 17 U.S.C. Section 107. 23. Retrieved online. 1 August 2021. https://commons.wikimedia.org/wiki/File:Wabash_Avenue_YMCA_Chicago_I

L.jpg

Back Cover

Photo of National Afro American Musuem & Cultural Center in Wilberforce, Ohio. Image available on the Internet and included in accordance with Title 17 U.S.C. Section 107. 23. Retrieved online. 27 March 2021. https://www.ohiohistory.org/visit/museum-and-site-locator/national-afro-american-museum

REFERENCES

About the Author

Jimmy Lee Tillman II, born on the Southside of Chicago in the aftermath of the assassination of Rev. Dr. Martin Luther King, Jr., to a civil rights veteran mother and world-renowned musician/educator father, is a history enthusiast and patriot. An alumnus of Central State University, who studied under the distinguished Black American History instructors, Professor Amos Martin and Dr. Joseph Lewis. Tillman is the founder and president of the Martin Luther King Republicans, Heritage Foundation Academy Fellow and producer of the Jimmy Lee Underground Radio Network. He is the father of three, pawpaw of one, and lives with his family in Chicago, Illinois.

You can connect with me on:
🌐 http://www.tillmanfamilypress.com

www.ingramcontent.com/pod-product-compliance
Lightning Source LLC
Chambersburg PA
CBHW050337230426
43663CB00010B/1889